CW00959439

OCCUPATIONAL SOURCES
FOR
GENEALOGISTS

A BIBLIOGRAPHY

by

STUART A. RAYMOND

Published by the
Federation of Family History Societies (Publications) Ltd.,
The Benson Room, Birmingham & Midlands Institute,
Margaret Street, Birmingham, B3 3BS, U.K.

Copies also available from:

S.A. & M.J. Raymond, 6, Russet Avenue, Exeter, Devon, EX1 3QB, U.K.

2nd edition

Cataloguing in publication data:

Raymond, Stuart A., 1945-. *Occupational Sources for genealogists: a bibliography.* 2nd ed. British genealogical bibliographies. Birmingham: Federation of Family History Societies, 1996.

DDC: 016.9293942

ISBN: 1-86006-36-6

ISSN: 1033-2065

Printed and bound by Oxuniprint, Walton Street, Oxford OX2 6DP

Introduction

A vast amount of occupational information of interest to genealogists is available in print. There are innumerable biographical dictionaries, descriptions of archives, record publications, lists of the members of professional societies, trade directories, genealogical guides, etc. All of these help us to identify people in the past, and may provide essential clues to tracing our family trees. The purpose of this bibliography is to draw these publications to the attention of genealogists. Arrangement is alphabetical by occupation; some general works are also included under headings such as "Business records" and "Trade union records'. The place of publication is London, except where otherwise indicated.

The term 'occupation' in the title of this bibliography has been interpreted broadly to include status as well. Hence titles relating to annuitants, book collectors, insurance policy holders, etc., have been included. In general, I have excluded works which are international in scope. I have also excluded works relating to occupations in a particular place; these are listed in the relevant county volumes of my *British genealogical bibliographies* series (see back cover). The number of works dealing with occupations in London is sufficiently large to warrant a separate book. London was (and still is) a magnet attracting workers from throughout Britain, and, even if you think you do not have London ancestors, you should still consult:

RAYMOND, STUART A. *Londoners' occupations: a genealogical guide.* F.F.H.S., 1994.

Well over 600 citations have been added to this edition. Nevertheless, I am conscious that I have still not achieved comprehensiveness. If you know of any useful works which I have missed, please let me know, so that they may be included in a third edition. In some instances, of course, whole books have been or could be written on sources for a particular occupation. Works on railwaymen, merchant seamen, and soldiers, amongst a number of others, are already available, and are noted below. When will someone tackle lawyers, Church of England clergymen, and landowners? Comprehensive treatment of occupations such as these could not be attempted here. For this edition, I have restricted the information concerning soldiers to guides compiled specifically for genealogists and other researchers, since the information I have in hand is sufficient to warrant a separate publication on this topic.

Many books on occupations simply describe a particular trade or craft, but give no information of direct genealogical value. Such works are excluded from this bibliography, since their inclusion would probably double the length. In any case, a useful bibliography already exists:

JEWELL, ANDREW. *Crafts, trades and industries: a book list for local historians.* National Council of Social Service, 1968.

Jewell aimed to list 'sources of information about the tools, processes, development and working conditions of the traditional crafts, trades and industries', according to his introduction. Direct information concerning many traditional trades and crafts is provided by:

HURLEY, BERYL, ed. *The book of trades or library of useful arts, 1811.* 3 vols. Keevil: Wiltshire Family History Society, 1991-4.

This was originally published in 1811, but its interest to genealogists is such that the Wiltshire Family History Society has re-issued it in a modern edition. Three dictionaries of historic occupations have been published recently:

CULLING, JOYCE. *An introduction to occupations: a preliminary list.* F.F.H.S., 1994.

TWINING, ANDREW, & TWINING, SANDRA. *Dictionary of old trades and occupations.* Kogarah, N.S.W.: the authors, 1993. Probably the most generally useful dictionary of occupations.

SCHLEBECKER, JOHN T. *The many names of country people: an historical dictionary from the twelfth century onwards.* New York: Greenwood Press, 1989. Dictionary of occupations, more extensive than the others, but more narrowly focused.

There are innumerable trade directories relating to particular occupations. Many are listed below, but others may be identified in two works:

SHAW, G., & TIPPER, A. *British directories: a bibliography and guide to directories published in England and Wales (1850-1950) and Scotland (1773-1950).* Leicester University Press, 1988.

MURPHY, SHEILA, & HENDERSON, CRISPIN A., ed. *Current British directories: a guide to directories published in the British Isles.* 12th ed. Beckenham: C.B.D. Research, 1993. First edition published 1953; earlier editions may be useful.

Biographical dictionaries relating to specific occupations are also numerous. These generally provide brief biographies of the persons included, and many are listed below. In general, however, biographical dictionaries which are international in scope have been excluded. They may be identified in:

SLOCUM, ROBERT B. *Biographical dictionaries and related works.* Detroit: Michigan, 1967. See also supplements 1972 and 1978.

The first edition of this book was based almost entirely on resources available to me in the libraries of Exeter. For this edition, I have used many other libraries, especially in London. The great majority of the works listed are widely available in reference libraries — although a few of the older items found in the British Library may be unique to that library. If the particular item you require is not available in your local library, you should ask the librarian to obtain it for you on inter-library loan, or at least to tell you where you can obtain a copy. Any reference library should be able to provide the latter information.

In compiling this bibliography, I have received assistance from a number of sources. Jeremy Gibson's suggestion that we should include more occupational information in our (then) joint publication, *English genealogy: an introductory bibliography,* provided the inspiration for this volume, when it became clear that far more occupational information was available in print than could reasonably be included in that work. I have used extensively the resources of Devon County Library, Exeter University Library, and the Devon and Exeter Institution. In London, the British Library, the Society of Genealogists, and Guildhall Library have all contributed many citations. Many other libraries have also been visited, too many to mention here. Cynthia Hanson and Paul Raymond have assisted me with the task of typing, and Brian Christmas has again been responsible for proof-reading. Bob Boyd has seen the book through the press. All of these people and institutions deserve my thanks. Any errors that remain — and I am sure there will be some — are my sole responsibility, and I would be grateful if they could be brought to my notice.

Stuart A. Raymond

Accountants

HABGOOD, WENDY, ed. *Chartered accountants in England and Wales: a guide to historical records.* Manchester: Manchester University Press, 1994. Lists the archives of individual firms — including names of founders and some partners — and of the Institute of Chartered Accountants and its predecessors, which includes membership records.

PARKER, R.H. *British accountants: a bibliographical sourcebook.* New York: Arno Press, 1980. Includes 65 lives, 19-20th c.

ASSOCIATION OF CERTIFIED AND CORPORATE ACCOUNTANTS. *List of members.* The Association, 1907- . Every 2-3 years.

INSTITUTE OF CHARTERED ACCOUNTANTS IN ENGLAND AND WALES. *List of members ...* The Institute, 1896- . Title varies.

INSTITUTION OF CERTIFIED PUBLIC ACCOUNTANTS. *List of members; extracts from the articles and bye-laws.* Edward Howlett, 1905. Lists 73 members only.

SOCIETY OF ACCOUNTANTS AND AUDITORS. *List of members, extracts from the articles, and bye-laws.* Henry Good & Son, 1888-1903. Title varies; continued by: *The Incorporated Accountants year book ...* Society of Incorporated Accountants and Auditors, 1888-1949. Title varies. Continued by *Society of Incorporated Accountants and Auditors list of members.* 1950- . Includes lists of members.

With the colours: a list of chartered and incorporated accountants and their clerks who are serving with the British forces on land and sea, 1914-1916. Gee & Co., 1916. Lists names, firms, and force joined.

Actors

For brief general discussions of sources of information, see:

BULLOCH, J.M. 'Theatrical families', *Genealogists' magazine* **6**, 1932-4, 339-47.

TAPPER, OSCAR. 'The history of local theatre', *Amateur historian* **6**(1), 1963, 22-4.

Several good bibliographies of theatrical literature are available:

ARNOTT, JAMES FULLARTON, & ROBINSON, JOHN WILLIAM. *English theatrical literature, 1559-1900: a bibliography.* Society for Theatre Research, 1970. Includes over 1400 citations to biographical works.

BENTLEY, GERALD EADES. *The Jacobean and Caroline stage.* 7 vols. Oxford: Clarendon Press, 1941-68. v.2. is a biographical dictionary of actors and actresses, v.3-5 is a bio-bibliography of playwrights.

CAVANAGH, JOHN. *British Theatre: a bibliography, 1901-1985.* Mottisfont: Motley Press, 1989. Includes over 3500 citations to works on theatrical and dramatic biography and criticism.

LOEWENBERG, ALFRED. *The theatre of the British Isles, excluding London: a bibliography.* Society for Theatre Research 1950. For provincial theatres.

WEARING, J.P. *American and British theatrical biography: a directory.* Metuchen: Scarecrow Press, 1979. Index to a wide range of biographical sources.

Many biographical dictionaries and directories are available; these include:

BAKER, DAVID ERSKINE, REED, ISAAC, & JONES, STEPHEN. *Biographia dramatica, or, a companion to the play house, containing historical and critical memoirs, and original anecdotes, of British and Irish dramatic writers, from the commencement of our theatrical exhibitions, among whom are some of the most celebrated actors ...* 3 vols. Longman, Guest, Rees Orme, and Browne, et al, 1812. Reprinted New York: AMS Press, 1966.

BALDWIN, THOMAS WHITFIELD. *The organization and personnel of the Shakespearean Company.* New York: Russell & Russell, 1927. Includes many names of actors.

BUSBY, ROY. *British music hall: an illustrated who's who from 1850 to the present day.* Paul Elek, 1976. Detailed biographies; unfortunately, they exclude information about private lives.

CLARKE, J.F. *Pseudonyms.* Elm Tree Books, 1977. Of actors, authors, *etc.*

DOUGLAS, ALBERT. *The amateurs' handbook and entertainers' directory, 1897.* Albert Douglas, 1897. Continued by: *Douglas's directory.* 1898-1914. Annual. Lists entertainers, vocalists, *etc.,* also theatrical tradesmen.

The dramatic and musical directory of the United Kingdom: the managers guide, theatrical register, and handbook to the provinces. The Proprietors, 1883-93. Annual. Includes lists of actors, directors, vocalists, *etc.,* also includes lists of proprietors of 'theatrical hotels' and 'professional lodgings'.

FLEAY, FREDERICK GARD. *A biographical chronicle of the English drama, 1559-1642.* 2 vols. Reeves & Turner, 1891. Reprinted New York: Lenox Hill, 1969.

Garraways directory of concert and variety artistes ... Garraway, 1934-9. 5 issues, title varies. List, with addresses.

The green register 1946-7: a comprehensive index and register of theatrical artists of stage, screen, radio, music, covering the United Kingdom of Great Britain and Northern Ireland, and Eire ... Putnam & Du Bree, [1947]

The green room book, or, who's who on the stage: an annual biographical record of the dramatic, musical and variety world. T. Sealy Clark. 1906-9. Annual.

HIGHFILL, PHILIP H., BURNIM, KALMAN A., & LANGHANS, EDWARD A. *A biographical dictionary of actors, actresses, musicians, dancers, managers and other stage personnel in London, 1660-1800.* 12 vols. Carbondale: Southern Illinois U.P., 1973. Biographical notes on 8,500 individuals.

Managers' hand-book of vocalists, instrumentalists, entertainers, orchestras, etc. Concorde Concert Control, 1899. Lists performers who could be hired from the publisher.

MULLIN, DONALD. *Victorian actors and actresses in review: a dictionary of contemporary views of representative British and American actors and actresses, 1837-1901.* Westport: Greenwood Press, 1983. Critics remarks on 234 actors and actresses.

MURRAY, JOHN TUCKER. *English dramatic companies 1558-1642.* 2 vols. Constable & Co., 1910. v.1. London companies, 1558-1642. v.2. Provincial companies, 1558-1642; appendices. Includes many names of actors, *etc.*

NUNGEZER, EDWIN. *A dictionary of actors and of other persons associated with the public representation of plays in England before 1642.* New Haven, Yale U.P., 1929. Reprinted New York: Greenwood Press, 1968.

PALMER, SCOTT. *A who's who of British film actors.* Metuchen: Scarecrow, 1981. Lists 14,000 British actors, with notes on their films.

ROOM, ADRIAN. *Naming names: a book of pseudonyms and name changes, with a who's who.* Routledge Kegan Paul, 1981. Includes many actors, artists, authors, playwrights, *etc.*

Who's who in the theatre 1912-1976: a biographical dictionary of actors, actresses, directors, playwrights and producers of the English speaking theatre ... 4 vols. Detroit: Gale Research, 1978. Notes on 4,100 individuals.

Who's who in the theatre: a biographical record of the contemporary stage. Sir Isaac Pitman, 1912- . Publisher varies; 17 editions to date.

Primary sources of the 17th century are available in a number of publications:

ADAMS, JOSEPH QUINCY. *The dramatic records of Sir Henry Herbert, master of the revels, 1623-1673.* New Haven: Yale University Press, 1917. Transcripts of play and play house licences and other dramatic records, many names of playwrights, theatre managers and others connected with the theatre.

CHAMBERS, E.K., & GREG, W.W. 'Royal patents for players', *Malone Society collections* 1(3), 1909, 260-84. 16-17th c.

'Dramatic records in the declared accounts of the Treasurer of the Chamber, 1558-1642', *Malone Society collections* 6, 1961 (1962), 1-178. Includes brief biographical notes on many actors.

HONIGMANN, E.A.J., & BROCK, SUSAN, eds. *Playhouse wills 1558-1642: an edition of wills by Shakespeare and his contemporaries in the London theatre.* Manchester: Manchester University Press, 1992.

STREITBERGER, W. *Jacobean and Caroline revels accounts, 1603-1642.* Malone Society collections 13. 1986.

Admiralty Officials
See Naval officials

Advertising Agents
Who's who in British advertising. Gainsborough, 1924-7. 3 issues.

Advocates
See Lawyers

Airmen
The aeroplane directory of British aviation
English Universities Press for Temple Press,
1928-48. Title and publisher varies; became
Who's who in aviation and, from 1936,
Who's who in British aviation.
*The aviation world who's who and industrial
directory.* 4 vols. Aviation World
Publishing Co., 1911-18. Includes some
portraits.

Airmen (R.A.F. etc.)
There are two important guides to sources
for airmen:
FOWLER, SIMON. *R.A.F. records in the P.R.O.*
P.R.O. readers guide **8.** P.R.O.Publications,
1994.
WILSON, EUNICE. *The records of the Royal
Air Force: how to find the few.*
Birmingham: F.F.H.S., 1991.
See also:
HURST, NORMAN. 'Royal Naval Air Service',
Family tree magazine **10**(3), 1994, 8-9.
HURST, NORMAN. 'When Pontius was a pilot',
Family tree magazine **8**(7), 1992, 23. Notes
on books relating to pilots of the Royal
Flying Corps and the early R.A.F.
In order to identify particular squadrons,
consult:
HALLEY, JAMES J. *The squadrons of the
Royal Air Force & Commonwealth, 1918-
1988.* Tonbridge: Air Britain, 1988.
Official lists of the R.A.F. include:
Lists of officers of the Royal Air Force.
J.B.H., 1985. Facsimile reprint of the edition
corrected to 1 April 1918.
The Air Force list, October 1940 ... H.M.S.O.,
1940. Reprinted Polstead: J.B.Hayward &
Son, 1990.
The monthly Air Force list. H.M.S.O., 1919- .
The volumes for the war years were
restricted.
For the First World War, see also:
CAMPBELL, G.L., & BLINKTHORN, R.H. *Royal
Flying Corps, Military wing: casualties and
honours during the war of 1914-17.* Picture
Advertising Co., 1917. Reprinted
Chippenham: Picton Print, 1987. Includes
much biographical information.

CAMPBELL, G.L. *Royal Flying Corps ...
casualties and honours during the war of
1914-17.* Picture Advertising Co., 1917.
Includes brief biographical notes.
HOBSON, CHRIS. *Airmen died in the Great War,
1914-1918: the roll of honour of the British
and Commonwealth air services of the First
World War.* J.B.Hayward & Son, 1995.
MCINNES, I. & WEBB, J.V. *A contemptible little
Flying Corps, being a definitive and
previously non-existent roll of those warrant
offices, N.C.O.'s and airmen who served in
the Royal Flying Corps prior to the outbreak
of the First World War.* London Stamp
Exchange, 1991.
WILLIAMSON, H.J. *The roll of honour: Royal
Flying Corps and Royal Air Force for the
Great War 1914-18.* Dallington: Naval &
Military Press, 1992.
For the Second World War, see:
CHORLEY, W.R. *Royal Air Force Bomber
Command losses of the Second World War.*
Leicester: Midland Counties Publications,
1992-4. v.1. Aircraft and crews lost during
1939-40; v.2. Aircraft and crew losses 1941;
v.3. Aircraft and crew losses, 1942.
PHILLIPS, J. ALWYN. *The valley of the shadow
of death: an account of the Royal Air Force
Bomber Command night bombing and
minelaying operations, including 'The Battle
of the Ruhr', March 5/6th to July 18/19th,
1943.* New Malden: Air Research
Publications, 1992. Gives names of many
crew.
WYNN, KENNETH G. *Men of the Battle of
Britain: a who was who of the pilots and
aircrew, British, Commonwealth and allied,
who flew with Royal Air Force Fighter
Command July 10 to Oct 31, 1940.* Norwich:
Gliddon Books 1989. Supplementary volume
1992.
Works on medals include:
TAVENDER, I.T. *The Distinguished Flying
Medal: a record of courage, 1918-1982.*
Polstead: J.B.Hayward & Son, 1990. List of
recipients, with notes.
[DICKSON, W.C.] *Seedies list of Fleet Air Arm
awards, 1939-1969.* [Tisbury]: Ripley Registers,
1990
COOPER, ALAN W. *In action with the enemy:
the holders of the Conspicuous Gallantry
Medal (Flying).* William Kimber, 1986.

MCINNES, IAN. *The Meritorious Service Medal to aerial forces.* Chippenham: Picton Publishing, 1984. Lists recipients.

BARNETT, GILBERT. *V.C's of the air: the glorious record of men of the British Empire Air Force awarded the Victoria Cross for valour ...* Ed. J.Burrow & Co., [1918]

BOWYER, CHAZ. *For valour: the air V.C's.* W. Kimber, 1978. R.A.F. medallists of both world wars.

JOHNS, WILLIAM EARL. *The air V.C's.* John Hamilton, [1935]. For 1915-19.

TURNER, JOHN FRAYN. *V.C's of the air.* George G. Harrop, 1960. How 32 V.C's were won in the Second World War.

IMPERIAL WAR GRAVES COMMISSION. *1939-1945: The Runnymede memorial to airmen who have no known grave.* Introduction + 14 pts. The Commission, 1953. Reprinted with amendments, Maidenhead: Commonwealth War Graves Commission, 1981-9.

Aldermen

See Mayors and Aldermen.

Almoners

TANNER, LAWRENCE E. 'Lord High Almoners and sub-almoners, 1100-1957', *Journal of the British Archeaological Association* 3rd series, 21, 1958, 72-83. List with brief biographical notes.

Annuitants

LEESON, FRANCIS. *A guide to the records of the British state tontines and life annuities of the seventeenth and eighteenth centuries.* Pinhorns handbooks, 3. Shalfleet, I.O.W.: Pinhorns, 1968. These records supply the age, parentage, residence, and dates of death, of thousands of late 17th — early 19th c. annuitants.

'The government life annuity of 1745', *Blackmansbury* 5(1-2), 1968, supplement, 1-42.

A list of the names of such proprietors of annuities, transferable at the South Sea House as were entitled to dividends on or before the 5th July 1837, and which remained unpaid on the 10th of October 1842. H. Teape and Son, [1842].

Apothecaries

BURNBY, JUANITA G.L. *A study of the English apothecary from 1660 to 1760.* Wellcome Institute for the History of Medicine, 1983. Includes pedigrees of the Conyers of Wakerly, Northamptonshire, Blaston, Leicestershire, and London; the Dickensons of Acton Trussell, Staffordshire and Newport, Shropshire, and the Gresleys of Bristol.

A list of persons who have obtained certificates of their fitness and qualification to practise as apothecaries from August 1, 1815 to July 31, 1840 ... Gilbert & Rivington, 1840.

Apprentices

Unpublished finding aids for genealogical research, series two: The Society of Genealogists apprenticeship index. 138 microfiche. Brighton: Harvester Press Microform, 1985. Important index to Inland Revenue records of apprenticeship indentures, 1710-62; lists apprentices and masters.

ARNOLD, ARTHUR P. 'Apprentices of Great Britain 1710-1773', *The Jewish Historical Society of England transactions* 22, 1968-9, 145-57. List of Jewish apprentices.

CAMP, A.J. 'Was he apprenticed?', *Family tree magazine* 1(3), 1985, 8-9.

GOLLAND, J.M. 'Compell'd to weep ... : the apprenticeship system', *Genealogists' magazine* 23(4), 1989, 121-7. General discussion of sources.

KETCHLEY, C.P. 'Apprentices: trade and poor', *Amateur historian* 2(12), 1956, 357-61.

THOMAS, E.G. 'Pauper apprenticeship', *Local historian* 14(7), 1981, 400-6. General discussion.

Architects

A number of general guides to sources for architects and architectural history are available; these include:

COLVIN, H.M. *English architectural history: a guide to sources.* 2nd ed. Pinhorns, 1976. General discussion, classifying potential sources of information. Originally published in *Archives* 2(14), 1955, 300-11.

HARVEY, JOHN H. 'Architectural archives', *Archives* 2, 1953-6, 117-22.

Architects *continued*

KAMEN, RUTH. *British and Irish architectural history: a bibliography and guide to sources of information.* Architectural Press, 1981.

MACE, ANGELA. *The Royal Institute of British Architects: a guide to its archive and history.* Mansell, 1986. "A considerable amount of biographical information on over 40,000 architects is available in the archive" — introduction. See also:

BASSETT, PHILIPPA. *Lists of historical records retained by the Royal Institute of British Architects.* Birmingham: Centre for Urban and Regional Studies; Reading: Institute of Agricultural History, 1980. The archives include registers of probationers and students, nomination forms, examination records, *etc.* likely to give much information on individual architects.

WODEHOUSE, L. *British architects 1840-1976: a guide to information sources.* Detroit: Gale Research, 1978.

Quite a number of biographical dictionaries and other lists of architects have been published. The following listing is arranged alphabetically by author:

ARCHITECTURAL PUBLICATION SOCIETY. *Dictionary of architecture.* 8 vols. Richards, [1852]-1892.

CHANCELLOR, EDWIN BERESFORD. *The lives of British architects from William of Wykeham to Sir William Chambers.* Duckworth & Co., 1909. Lives of prominent architects.

COLVIN, H.M. *A biographical dictionary of British architects, 1600-1840.* Rev. ed. John Murray, 1978. The standard work.

FELSTEAD, ALISON, FRANKLIN, JONATHAN, & PINFIELD, LESLIE. *Directory of British architects, 1834-1900.* Mansell, 1993. Extensive; sponsored by the Royal Architectural Library and the Royal Institute of British Architects.

FREEMAN, ALBERT C. *The architects and surveyors directory & referendum.* John W.Marks, 1907-12. Includes directories of architects, builders', electrical contractors, *etc.*

GRAY, A.STUART. *Edwardian architecture: a biographical dictionary.* Duckworth, 1985.

HARRIS, EILEEN. *British architectural books and writers, 1556-1785.* Cambridge: Cambridge University Press, 1990. Biographical dictionary.

HARVEY, JOHN. *English medieval architects: a biographical dictionary down to 1550, including master masons, carpenters, carvers, building contractors, and others responsible for design.* 2nd ed. Gloucester: Alan Sutton, 1984. The standard work.

ROYAL INSTITUTE OF BRITISH ARCHITECTS. *List of members, contributors to the collection and library, proceedings ...* The Institute, 1871-9. Annual?

ROYAL INSTITUTE OF BRITISH ARCHITECTS. *The kalendar.* The Institute, 1885- . Includes lists of members, fellows, associates, officers, *etc.*

ROYAL INSTITUTE OF BRITISH ARCHITECTS. *Register of fellows, associates and students.* 1905-38. Continued as *Register of fellows and associates,* 1948-60, and as *Register of corporate members,* 1964- . Originally listed in the *Proceedings* of the Institute.

WARE, DORA. *A short dictionary of British architects.* George Allen & Unwin, 1967.

The architects, engineers and building trades directory. Wyman & Sons, 1868. Includes many biographical notes.

Who's who in architecture, giving brief biographies and other useful particulars of architects practising in the United Kingdom. Technical Journals, 1914.

See also Artists and Builders

Artists

AUERBACH, ERNA. *Tudor artists: a study of painters in the royal service and of portaiture on illuminated documents from the accession of Henry VIII to the death of Elizabeth I.* Athlone Press, 1954. Includes list of artists patronised by the royal court, with biographical notes.

BROOK-HART, DENYS. *20th century British marine painting.* Woodbridge: Antique Collectors Club, 1981. Includes 'guide to marine artists, c.1900-1980'.

BRYAN, MICHAEL. *Bryan's dictionary of painters and engravers.* 5 vols. New ed. George Bell, 1903-5.

BURBIDGE, R. BRINSLEY. *A dictionary of British flower, fruit and still life painters.* 2 vols. Leigh on Sea: F. Lewis, 1974. Vol.1. 1515-1849. Vol.2. 1850-1950.

CLAYTON, EILEEN CREATHORNE. *English female artists.* 2 vols. Tinsley Bros., 1876. Many biographical sketches, 16-19th c.

CUNNINGHAM, ALLAN. *The lives of the most eminent British painters, sculptors, and architects.* 3 vols. Rev. ed., by Mrs Charles Heaton. George Bell & Sons, 1879-80.

DOLMAN, BERNARD. *A dictonary of contemporary British artists, 1929.* 2nd ed., Woodbridge: Antique Collectors Club, 1981. Originally published Art Trade Press, 1929. Includes 4,450 entries.

FINCHAM, HENRY W. *Artists and engravers of British and American book plates: a book of reference for book plate and print collectors.* Kegan Paul, Trench, Trübner & Co., 1897. Extensive listing.

FISHER, STANLEY W. *A dictionary of watercolour painters, 1750-1900.* W.Foulsham & Co., 1972.

FOSKETT, D. *British portrait miniatures: a history.* Spring Books, 1963. Includes information on the miniaturists.

FOSKETT, DAPHNE. *Miniatures: dictionary and guide.* Woodbridge: Antique Collectors Club, 1979.

FOSTER, JOSHUA JAMES. *A dictionary of painters of miniatures (1525-1850), with some account of exhibitions, collections, sales, etc., pertaining to them,* ed. Ethel M. Foster. Philip Allan, 1936.

FRIEND, G.W. *Index of painters and engravers, with the titles of their works, declared at the office of the Printsellers Association ... as described in an 'Alphabetical list of engravings.'* Printsellers Association, 1894. For the period 1847-93.

GILBEY, WALTER, SIR. *Animal painters of England from the year 1650: a brief history of their lives and works ...* 3 vols. Vinton & Co., 1910-11. Biographical dictionary.

GRANT, MAURICE HAROLD. *A chronological history of the old English landscape painters (in oils) from the XVIth century to the XIXth century.* 3 vols. Leigh on Sea: F Lewis, 1926-47. Notices of some 500 painters, many obscure.

GRANT, MAURICE HAROLD. *A dictionary of British landscape painters from the 16th century to the early 20th century.* Leigh on Sea: F Lewis, 1952. Brief biographical notes.

GRAVES, ALGERNON. *The British Institution, 1806-1867: a complete dictionary of contributors and their work from the foundation of the Institution.* George Bell & Sons, 1908.

GRAVES, ALGERNON. *A century of loan exhibitions.* 3 vols. Bath: Kingsmead Reprint, 1970. Originally published 1913-15. Lists artists and their work, with places and dates of exhibitions.

GRAVES, ALGERNON. *A dictionary of artists who have exhibited works in the principal London exhibitions from 1760 to 1893.* 3rd ed. H. Graves & Co., 1901. Reprinted Bath: Kingsmead Reprints, 1970. List of names, with residence, dates and speciality.

GRAVES, ALGERNON. *The Royal Academy of Arts: a complete dictionary of contributors and their works from its foundation in 1769 to 1904.* 8 vols. H. Graves & Co., 1905-6. Reprinted in 4 vols East Ardsley: S.R. Publishers, 1970. Includes addresses, lists of works, and dates.

GRAVES, ALGERNON. *The Society of Artists of Great Britain, 1760-1791, the Free Society of Artists, 1761-1783: a complete dictionary of contributors and their work from the foundation of the societies to 1791.* G. Bell & Sons, 1907. Reprinted Bath: Kingsmead Reprints, 1970. Includes addresses, lists of works, and dates.

JOHNSON, J., & GREUTZNER, A. *A dictionary of British artists, 1880-1940.* Woodbridge: Antique Collectors Club, 1976. Lists 41,000 artists, with brief biographical notes.

LAMBOURNE, LIONEL, & HAMILTON, JEAN. *British watercolours in the Victoria and Albert Museum: an illustrated summary catalogue of the national collection.* Sotheby Parke Bernet, 1980. Includes biographical notes on artists.

LEWIS, FRANK. *A dictionary of British historical painters.* Leigh on Sea: F. Lewis, 1979. Brief biographical notes.

LONG, BASIL. *British miniaturists.* [New ed.] Holland Press, 1966. Detailed biographical notes.

MALLALIEU, H.L. *The dictionary of British watercolour artists up to 1920.* 2nd ed. 3 vols. Woodbridge: Antique Collectors Club, 1986-90. Brief biographies of c. 5,000 artists.

MAYNE, ARTHUR. *British profile miniaturists.* Faber & Faber, 1970.

Artists *continued*

MCKECHNIE, SUE. *British silhouette artists and their work, 1760-1860.* Sotheby Parke Bernet, 1978. Includes biographical notices.

MITCHELL, SALLY. *The dictionary of British equestrian artists.* Woodbridge: Antique Collectors Club, 1955. Brief biographies of 870 artists.

ORMOND, RICHARD, & ROGERS, MALCOLM. *Dictionary of British portraiture.* 4 vols. B.T. Batsford, 1979-81. Lists thousands of portraits, alphabetically by name of sitter.

OTTLEY, HENRY. *A biographical and critical dictionary of recent and living painters and engravers, forming a supplement to Bryan's dictionary of painters and engravers as edited by George Stanley.* George Ball & Sons, 1876.

PAVIERE, SYDNEY. *A dictionary of British flower, fruit and still life painters.* 3 vols. (including 2 separate vols. 2). Leigh on Sea: F. Lewis, 1974. Brief biographical notes.

PAVIERE, S.H. *A dictionary of British sporting painters.* 2nd ed. Leigh on Sea: F. Lewis, 1979.

PAVIERE, SYDNEY HERBERT. *A dictionary of Victorian landscape painters.* Leigh on Sea: F. Lewis, 1968. Brief notes on over 2,000 painters.

REDGRAVE, SAMUEL. *A dictionary of artists of the English school.* New ed. G. Bell & Sons, 1878. Includes 'painters, sculptors, architects, engravers and ornamentists.'

SANDBY, WILLIAM. *The history of the Royal Academy of Arts from its foundations in 1768 to the present time, with biographical notices of all its members.* 2 vols. Longmans Green, Longman, Roberts, & Green, 1862. Includes numerous biographies.

SPARROW, WALTER SHAW. *A book of sporting painters.* John Lane, the Bodley Head, 1931. Includes thirteen wills of leading painters, folded pedigree of Alken, 18th c., *etc.*

WATERHOUSE, ELLIS. *The dictionary of 16th & 17th century British painters.* Woodbridge: Antique Collectors' Club, 1988.

WATERS, GRANT M. *Dictionary of British artists working 1900-1950.* 2 vols. Eastbourne: Eastbourne Fine Art, 1975. Biographies of 5,500 artists.

WILLIAMSON, GEORGE C. *The miniature collector: a guide for the amateur collector of portrait miniatures.* Herbert Jenkins, 1921. Includes notes on many miniature painters.

WILSON, ARNOLD. *A dictionary of British marine painters.* Leigh on Sea: F. Lewis, 1967.

WINDSOR, ALAN, ed. *Handbook of modern British painting, 1900-1980.* Aldershot: Scholar Press, 1992. Biographical dictionary.

WOOD, CHRISTOPHER. *Dictionary of Victorian painters.* 2nd ed. Woodbridge: Antique Collectors' Club, 1978. Includes over 11,000 brief biographical notes.

WOOD, CHRISTOPHER. *Victorian painters.* 2 vols. Dictionary of British Art 4. Woodbridge: Antique Collectors' Club, 1995. Contents: v.1. The text. v.2. Historical survey and plates.

Royal Academy exhibitors, 1905-1970: a dictionary of artists and their work in the summer exhibitions of the Royal Academy of Arts. 6 vols. East Ardsley: E.P. Publishing, 1973-82. Lists artists with addresses, dates of exhibitions, etc.

Who's who in art. The Art Trade Press, 1927. Many subsequent editions. For contemporary artists.

Armourers

FFOULKES, CHARLES. *The armourer and his craft, from the XIth to the XVIth century.* Methuen & Co.., 1912. Includes list of English armourers.

Astronomers

DUNKIN, EDWIN. *Obituary notices of astronomers, fellows and associates of the Royal Astronomical Society ...* Williams & Norgate, 1879. 24 obituaries.

Attornies

See Lawyers

Auctioneers

ALLNUT, HENRY. *The Auctioneers, land agents, valuers and estate agents directory, showing the auctioneers (who sell land & houses) and land and estate agents throughout the Kingdom; also, drainage engineers ...* Estates Gazette, 1860-62. 2 Issues.

The Auctioneer's Institute of the United Kingdom ... yearbook containing list of members ... E.P.Wilson, 1892- . Title and

publisher varies; became The Chartered Auctioneers and Estate Agents Institute from 1948.
See also Surveyors

Authors

ALLIBONE, S. AUSTIN. *Critical dictionary of English literature and British and American authors, living and deceased, from the earliest accounts to the latter half of the nineteenth century.* 5 vols. Gale, 1965. Originally published Philadelphia: Lippincott, 1858-91; over 46,000 notices. Supplemented by:

KIRK, JOHN FOSTER. *A supplement to Allibone's critical dictionary of English literature and British and American authors.* 2 vols. Philadelphia: Lippincott, 1891. Reprinted Detroit: Gale, 1965.

ALSTON, ROBIN C. *A checklist of women writers 1801-1900: fiction, verse, drama.* British Library, 1990.

ATKINSON, FRANK. *Dictionary of literary pseudonyms: a selection of popular modern writers in English.* 2nd ed. Clive Bingley, 1977.

The authors and writers who's who, 1934. Shaw Publishing, 1934- .

A biographical dictionary of the living authors of Great Britain and Ireland, comprising literary memoirs and anecdotes of their lives, and a chronological register of their publications ... Henry Colburn, 1816.

BELL, MAUREEN, PARFITT, GEORGE, & SHEPHERD, SIMON. *A biographical dictionary of English women writers, 1580-1720.* New York: Harvester, 1990.

CROSS, NIGEL. *The Royal Literary Fund, 1790-1918: an introduction to the fund's history and archives, with an index of applicants.* World Microfilms Publications, 1984.

FENWICK, GILLIAN. *The contributor's index to the 'Dictionary of national biography', 1885-1901.* Winchester: St Paul's Bibliographies, 1989.

INGRAM, ALISON. *Index to the archives of Richard Bentley & Son, 1829-1898.* Cambridge: Chadwick-Henley, 1977. Index to the papers of a publisher; many authors named.

KAMM, ANTHONY. *Collins biographical dictionary of English literature.* Harper Collins, 1993.

KUNITZ, STANLEY J., & HAYCRAFT, HOWARD. *British authors before 1800: a biographical dictionary.* New York: H.W. Wilson & Co., 1952.

KUNITZ, STANLEY J. *British authors of the nineteenth century.* New York: H.W. Wilson, 1936. 1,000 biographies. Continued chronologically by the same author's *Twentieth century authors.* H.W. Wilson, 1942. Supplement, 1955.

The literary year book. George Alan, 1897-1923. Annual; publisher varies. Some issues include an extensive 'who's who in literature,' lists of booksellers, *etc.*

MYERS, ROBIN. *A dictionary of literature in the English language from Chaucer to 1940.* 2 vols. Oxford: Pergamon, 1970. Includes many brief biographical notes. A volume covering 1940-1970 was published 1978.

RUSSELL, JOSIAH COX. *Dictionary of writers of the thirteenth century.* Bulletin of the Institute of Historical Research, special supplement, 3. Longmans, Green & Co., 1936.

SHATTOCK, JOANE. *The Oxford guide to British women writers.* Oxford: O.U.P., 1993. Biographical dictionary.

TODD, JANET *Dictionary of British and American women writers, 1660-1800.* Methuen & Co., 1987.

Who was who in literature, 1906-1934. 2 vols. Detroit: Gale, 1979. Includes 10,400 entries.

Automobile Association Employees

BASSETT, PHILLIPPA. *List of the historical records of the Automobile Association.* Birmingham: University of Birmingham Center for Urban and Regional Studies/ Reading: Institute of Agricultural History, 1980. Some staff and membership records are listed.

Bank Stock Holders, *etc*

A list of the names of all the proprieters of the Bank of England, March 25, 1709. John Humphries, 1709.

The names and descriptions of the proprietors of unclaimed dividends on bank stock which became due before the 10th October 1780 and remained unpaid on the 30th September

1790. Bank of England, 1791. Similar lists are available for various years to 1843.

The unclaimed dividend books of the Bank of England, containing the names and descriptions of upwards of twenty thousand persons entitled to various sums of money of all amounts ... W.Strange, [1845?]

A list of the names of all proprietors of stock of the Bank of England qualified to vote at the ensuing election to be made of Governor & deputy governor, on Tuesday, April 2, 1889 ... Bank of England, 1889.

"Sephardic and other Jewish holders of Bank of England stock,' *Miscellanies of the Jewish Historical Society of England* **6**, 1962, 144-74. Lists.

Bankers and Bank Customers

ASHBEE, ROSEMARY. 'The archives of some great banking houses', *Genealogists' magazine* **17**, 1972-4, 213-7. General discussion.

CAMPBELL, JESSIE. 'Barclays bank archive,' *Manchester region history review* **4**(2), 1990/1, 42-6.

COLDICOTT, DIANA K. 'Researching a small private bank,' *Local history magazine* **51**, 1995, 14-16.

HART, RICHARD. *Lloyds Bank: a pictorial history with text and staff anecdotes.* Leighton Buzzard: Farnon Books, 1989. Includes staff list as at 1st January 1903, identifying 2,000 employees throughout the country.

MALCOLM, CHARLES A. *The history of the British Linen Bank.* Edinburgh: T. & A. Constable, 1950. Includes roll of honour, 1914-18, and 1939-45, and biographical notes on Union Staff.

PRESSNELL, L.S., & ORBELL, JOHN. *A guide to the historical records of British banking.* Aldershot: Gower, 1985. The standard guide; includes notes on the papers of banking families.

TWIGG, T. *Twiggs corrected list of the country-bankers of England and Wales, with the christian and surnames of all such as take out licenses for issuing promissory notes payable on demand.* T. Twigg, 1830.

The banking almanac, directory, and bankers year-book ... Richard Groombridge & Sons, 1845- . Title and publisher varies. Gives many names of partners, agents, managers etc.

A directory of the joint-stock & private banks in England and Wales 1851-1852, comprising a statistical account of every bank, lists of all the shareholders and private partners and a complete digest of banking law ... Richard Groombridge & Sons, 1852.

A return of the number of county banks issuing notes, which have become bankrupt, from January 1826 to the present time ... House of Commons Parliamentary Papers, 1833, **XXXI**, 199-203. Gives names of partners.

Bankruptcy Officers

Return of the names of all persons holding any office in the several courts of bankruptcy and insolvency in England and Wales ... House of Commons Parliamentary Papers, 1861, **LI**, 39-43. See also 1863, **XLVIII**, 171-3.

Bankrupts

For brief discussion of sources for bankrupts, see:

LAMBERT, DAVID. 'Was your ancestor a bankrupt?' *Family History Society of Cheshire journal* **22**(3), 1993, 13-14. Brief discussion of sources.

MARRINER, SHIELA. 'English bankruptcy records and statistics before 1850,' *Economic history review* 2nd series, **33**, 1980, 351-66. Includes discussion of bankruptcy records at the Public Record Office.

Various lists of bankrupts are available:

An alphabetical list of all the bankrupts, from the first of January, 1774 to the thirtieth of June 1786, inclusive, with the date of the certificates and supersedures to those who have received them. J.Jarvis, 1786.

BAILEY, WM. *Bailey's list of bankrupts' dividends and certificates, from the year 1772 to 1793, both included, with the names and residence of the different solicitors under each.* 2 vols. T.Wilkins, 1794.

The bankrupts register for the year 18--. 13 issues. School-Press, 1832-47.

Brough's alphabetical gazette: a permanent register of bankrupts, insolvents, assignments, sequestrations, dividends, certificates, partnership dissolutions, notable suspensions, etc, for the purposes of reference. W.J.Adams, 1861. This was intended to be continued quarterly, but only the first two parts were published.

ELWICK, GEORGE. *The bankrupt directory, being a complete register of all the bankrupts, with their residences, trades, and dates when they appeared in the London Gazette, from December 1820 to April 1843* ... Simpkin Marshall and Co.., 1843.

List of the bankrupts with their dividends and certificates for the year 1794. T.Wilkins, 1795. A further volume covers 1795.

Returns as to bankruptcies previous to the act of parliament 1831 ... House of Commons Parliamentary Papers, 1839, **XLIII,** 1-157. Gives names, residences, occupations, dates of bankruptcies, and financial details, from the late 18th c. to 1831.

Returns by each of the official assignees of the Court of Bankruptcy, and of the courts of the country districts, showing the names of every bankrupt ... under whose estate or estates any remuneration whatever has been allowed to the said official assignee, from the 1st day of January 1851 to the 31st day of December 1852 ... House of Commons Parliamentary Papers 1854, **LIII,** 247-353. Much more information is to be found in the Parliamentary Papers; the returns cited here are only examples.

SMITH, WILLIAM AND CO. *A list of bankrupts with their dividends, certificates, &c., &c., for the last twenty years and six months, viz from Jan 1, 1786 to June 24, 1806 inclusive* ... William Smith & Co., 1806. Extensive list.

Barometer Makers

BANFIELD, EDWIN. *Barometer makers and retailers, 1660-1900.* Trowbridge: Baros Books, 1991. Extensive listing.

BANFIELD, EDWIN. *The Italian influence on English barometers from 1780.* Trowbridge: Baros Books, 1993. General study.

GOODISON, NICHOLAS. *English barometers, 1680-1860: a history of domestic barometers and their makers.* New York: C.N. Potter, 1968. Includes list of makers, with biographical data.

Barristers

See Lawyers

Bellfounders and Bellringers

HOPE, R. C. 'English bellfounders, 1150-1893', *Archaeological journal* **50,** 1893, 150-75. List of names.

KETTERINGHAM, JOHN R. 'Dead ringers' (or campanological sources),' *Family tree magazine* **10**(5), 1994, 45.

MORRIS, ERNEST. 'British bellfounders, with a chronological list of all known names,' *Topographical quarterly* **4,** 1935-6, 72-87.

PAYNE, VALERIE M. 'Genealogy through campanology,' *West Middlesex Family History Society journal* **7**(3), 1988, 109-10. Brief discussion.

WALTERS, H.B. *Church bells of England.* Oxford: Oxford University Press, 1977. Reprinted East Ardsley: E P Publishing, 1977. Includes extensive lists of British bellfounders, much information on bell inscriptions, an extensive bibliography, *etc.*

Bio-Physical Assistants

SOCIETY OF APOTHECARIES OF LONDON. *Register of bio-physical assistants.* British Medical Association, 1931- . Annual.

Bishops and Archbishops

LE NEVE, JOHN. *The lives and characters, deaths, burials and epitaphs of all the Protestant bishops of the Church of England since the Reformation as settled by Queen Elizabeth, Anno Dom. 1559.* William & John Innys, 1720. vol.1. only published.

LOWNDES, FREDERICK SAWREY. *Bishops of the day: a biographical dictionary of all the bishops and archbishops of the Church of England and of all churches in communion therewith throughout the world.* Grant Richards, 1897.

STUBBS, WILLIAM. *Registrum sacrum Anglicanum: an attempt to exhibit the course of episcopal succession in England from the records and chronicles of the Church.* 2nd ed. Oxford: Clarendon Press, 1897. Gives dates of consecration.

'Appointments of Bishops and Archbishops on the Patent Rolls, Charles II,' *Forty-sixth annual report of the Deputy Keeper of the Public Records,* 1885, appendix I, 1-17.

Boatmen

WIDDOWSON, B. 'Old occupations: river sailor', *Family tree magazine* **10**(3), 1994, 43-4.

British Transport Commission Historical Records: canal, dock, harbour, navigation and steamships companies (RAIL 800-887). Class list. List & Index Society, **142**. 1977. Lists, amongst much else, staff records and share registers.

See also Canal Boatmen

Book Collectors

DAVENPORT, CYRIL. *English heraldic book-stamps.* Archibald Constable, 1909. Gives heraldic notes on book collectors. For corrections, see: CLEMENTS, H.J.B. 'Armorial book-stamps and their owners,' *The Library* 4th series, **20**(2), 1939, 121-35.

ELTON, CHARLES ISAAC, & ELTON, MARY AUGUSTA. *The great book-collectors.* Kegan Paul, Trench, Trübner & Co., 1893.

FLETCHER, WILLIAM YOUNGER. *English book collectors,* ed. Alfred Pollard. Kegan Paul, Trench, Trübner and Co., 1902. Biographies of many well-known book collectors.

ALLPRESS, PETER. 'Augmentations on armorial bookplates', *The bookplate journal* **5**(2), 1987, 53-89; **6**(2), 1988, 84-93.

HAZLITT, WILLIAM CAREW. *A roll of honour: a calendar of the names of over 17,000 men and women who, throughout the British Isles, and in our early colonies have collected maps and printed books, from the XIVth to the XIXth century, with topographical and personal notices and anecdotes of many of them ...* B. Quaritch, 1908. Reprinted New York: B. Franklin, 1971.

JAYNE, SEARS. *Library catalogues of the English Renaissance.* [2nd ed.] Godalming: St Pauls Bibliographies, 1983. Lists many inventories of book collectors.

LEE, BRIAN NORTH. *British bookplates: a pictorial history.* Newton Abbot: David & Charles, 1979. Includes notes on 261 book collectors; includes useful bibliography.

LEE, BRIAN NORTH. *Early printed book labels and gift labels printed in Britain to the year 1760.* Pinner: Private Libraries Association, 1976.

LATTIMORE, COLIN R. 'Heraldry and bookplates', *The bookplate journal* **2**(2), 1984, 61-74.

QUARITCH, BERNARD. *Contributions towards a dictionary of English book collectors ...* 14 parts. Bernard Quaritch, 1892-1921. Innumerable books list persons who have subscribed prior to publication. These subscription lists include many thousand names. For useful guides to them, see:

WALLIS, P.J. 'Book subscription lists,' *The Library* 5th series. **29**, 1974, 255-86. Preliminary survey.

ROBINSON, F.J.G., & WALLIS, P.J. *Book subscription lists: a revised guide.* Newcastle upon Tyne: Harold Hill and Son for the Book Subscription Lists Project, 1975.

WALLIS, P.J., & WALLIS, RUTH. *Book subscription lists: extended supplement to the revised guide.* Newcastle upon Tyne: Project for Historical Bibliography, 1996.

Book Illustrators

HORNE, ALAN. *The dictionary of 20th century British book illustrators.* Woodbridge: Antique Collectors Club, 1994.

Book Patrons

WILLIAMS, FRANKLIN B. *Index of dedications and commendatory verses in English books before 1641.* Bibliographical Society, 1962. Index of dedicatees.

Bookbinders

RAMSDEN, CHARLES. *Bookbinders of the United Kingdom (outside London), 1780-1840.* Privately printed, 1954. Brief notes on c. 3,000 bookbinders.

RAMSDEN, CHARLES. *London bookbinders, 1780-1840.* B.T. Batsford, 1956. Reprinted 1987. Detailed list of 2,000 names, including addresses.

Bookmakers

Directory of turf accountants and commission agents. 2 issues. Turf Guardian Society, 1921-2.

The Turf Guardian year book. Turf Guardian Society, 1927.

Booksellers, Printers and Publishers

In past times, these three trades were often performed by the same individual. Consequently, works relating to them are listed here together. The following list is in rough chronological order.

TIMPERLEY, C.H. *A dictionary of printers and printing, with the progress of literature, ancient and modern, bibliographical illustrations, etc. etc.* H.Johnson, 1839.

DUFF, E. GORDON. *A century of the English book trades: short notices of all printers, stationers, book-binders, and others connected with it from the issue of the first dated book in 1457 to the incorporation of the Company of Stationers in 1557.* Bibliographical Society, 1948.

POLLARD, A.W., & REDGRAVE, G.R. *A short title catalogue of books printed in England, Scotland and Ireland, and of English books printed abroad, 1475-1640.* 2nd ed. 3 vols. Bibliographical Society, 1986-91. v.3. includes a 'printers and publishers index'.

HUMPRHIES, CHARLES, & SMITH, WILLIAM C. *Music publishing in the British Isles, from the beginning until the middle of the nineteenth century: a dictionary of engravers, printers, publishers, and music sellers, with a historical introduction.* 2nd ed. Oxford: Basil Blackwell, 1970. Brief biographical information.

PLOMER, HENRY R. *Abstracts from the wills of English printers and stationers from 1492 to 1630.* Bibliographical Society, 1903.

WORMAN, ERNEST JAMES. *Alien members of the book trade during the Tudor period, being an index to those whose names occur in the returns of aliens, letters of denization and other documents published by the Huguenot Society.* Bibliographical Society, 1906.

Hand list of English printers, 1501-1556. 4 pts. London Bibliographical Society, 1895-1913.

MYERS, ROBIN. *Stationers Company archive 1554-1984: an account of the records.* St Pauls Bibliographies, 1990.

ARBER, EDWARD, ed. *A transcript of the registers of the Company of Stationers of London, 1554-1640, A.D.* 5 vols. Gloucester, Massachusetts: Peter Smith, 1967. Originally published 1875-95. Gives names of many printers, booksellers, etc. Three further volumes cover the period 1640-1708.

WILLIAMS, WILLIAM P. *Index to the Stationers registers, 1640-1708, being an index to a transcript of the registers of the Worpshipful Company of Stationers from 1640-1708, edited by Eyre, Rivington and Plomer, (1913-1914).* La Jolla, California: Laurence McGilvery, 1980. Includes 2 fiche.

GREG, W.W. *Licensers for the press, &c., to 1640: a biographical index based mainly on Arber's Transcript of the Registers of the Company of Stationers.* Oxford Bibliographical Society Publications, N.S., 10. 1962.

GREG, W.W., & BUSWELL, E. *Records of the court of the Stationers Co., 1576 to 1602, from register B.* Bibliographical Society, 1930. Gives many names.

JACKSON, WILLIAM A., ed. *Records of the court of the Stationers Company, 1602-1640.* Bibliographical Society, 1957.

MCKENZIE, D.F. 'A list of printers' apprentices, 1605-1640,' *Studies in bibliography* 13, 1960, 109-42. From the records of the Stationers Company of London; apprentices were recruited from throughout the country.

MCKERROW, R.B., ed. *A dictionary of printers and booksellers in England, Scotland and Ireland, and of foreign printers of English books, 1557-1640.* Bibliographical Society, 1910.

MORRISON, PAUL G. *Index of printers, publishers and booksellers in Donald Wing's 'Short title catalogue of books ... 1641-1700'.* Charlottesville: University of Virginia Press, 1955.

PLOMER, HENRY R. *Dictionary of the booksellers and printers who were at work in England, Scotland and Ireland from 1641 to 1667.* Bibliographical Society, 1907.

PLOMER, HENRY ROBERT. *A dictionary of the printers and booksellers who were at work in England, Scotland and Ireland from 1668 to 1725,* ed. Arundell Esdaile. Oxford: Oxford U.P., 1922.

MAXTED, IAN. *The British book trades 1710-1777: an index of the masters and apprentices recorded in the Inland Revenue registers at the Public Record Office, Kew.* Exeter working papers in British book trade history, 2. Exeter: J.Maxted, 1983.

PLOMER, H.R., et al. *A dictionary of the printers and booksellers who were at work in England, Scotland and Ireland from 1726 to 1775.* Oxford: O.U.P., for the Bibliographical Society, 1932.

MORTIMER, RUSSELL S. 'Biographical notices of printers and publishers of Friends' books up to 1750: a supplement to Plomer's Dictionary', *Journal of documentation* 3(2), 1947, 107-25.

Booksellers, *etc., continued*

TODD, WILLIAM B., & WALLIS, PETER J. 'Provincial booksellers c.1744: the *Harleian miscellany* subscription list,' *The Library* 5th series **29**, 1974, 422-40. List.

'Quaker printers, 1750-1850,' *Journal of the Friends Historical Society* **50**(3), 1963, 100-33. Includes list.

MAXTED, IAN. *The British book trades, 1775-1787: an index to insurance policies.* Exeter working papers in British book trade history **8**. Exeter: J.Maxted, 1992.

PENDRED, JOHN. *The earliest directory of the book trade,* ed Graham Pollard. Supplement to the *Bibliographical Society's transactions* **14**. 1955. Originally published 1785.

FEATHER, JOHN. *The English provincial book trade before 1850: a checklist of secondary sources.* Oxford Bibliographical Society occasional publication, **16**. Oxford: the Society, 1981. Lists many biographical sources relating to particular counties.

Hodson's booksellers, publishers and stationers directory 1855: a facsimile of the copy in the Bodleian Library, Oxford, with an introduction by Graham Pollard. Occasional publication, **7**. Oxford Bibliographical Society, 1972.

GYLES, ARTHUR. *The directory of second-hand booksellers.* Nottingham: Arthur Gyles, 1886.

PARKINSON, JOHN A. *Victorian music publishers: an annotated list.* Michigan: Harmonie Park Press, 1990. Brief notes on professional activities.

Kelly's directory of stationers, printers, booksellers and papermakers of England, Scotland, and Wales ... Kelly & Co., 1872-1939. 20 issues.

MEREDITH, MARK. *British booksellers.* Liverpool: Literary Yearbooks Press, 1924. Continues section of *The literary yearbook.*

See also Authors

Botanists

ALLEN, DAVID ELLISTON. *The botanists: a history of the Botanical Society of the British Isles through a hundred and fifty years.* Winchester: St Pauls Bibliographies, 1986. Includes list of members.

BRITTEN, JAMES & BOULGER, GEORGE S. *A biographical index of British and Irish botanists.* 2nd ed. Taylor & Francis, 1931. Includes brief biographical notices.

DESMOND, RAY. *Dictionary of British and Irish botanists and horticulturists, including plant collectors and artists.* 3rd ed. Taylor & Francis, 1977. Over 10,000 brief biographies.

GUNTHER, R.T. *Early British botanists and their gardens, based on unpublished writings of Goodyer, Tradescant and others.* Oxford: O.U.P., 1922. Includes 'Notes on contemporary botanists.'

Brass Rubbers

BUSBY, RICHARD J. *A companion guide to brasses and brass rubbing.* Pelham Books, 1973. Includes as an appendix the extensive 'Who was who in brass rubbing: a bio-bibliographical guide.'

Breeders

Lang's breeders directory 1912. R.T. Lang, 1912. Lists breeders of bees, cattle, dogs, goats, horses, pigs, pigeon, poultry, rabbits and sheep.

TOLL, R.D.E. *Tillotson's directory of pedigree stock breeders, and year book of the breeding industry ... 1926-7.* Tillotson's Publishing, 1926. Continued by: TOLL, R.D.E. *International directory of pedigree stock breeders ...* Vernon Press, 1928-30. 2 issues. Lists breeders of cattle, sheep, pigs and horses throughout Great Britain, as well as overseas.

Brewers

The standard guide to brewing archives *etc.,* is:

RICHMOND, LESLEY M., & TURTON, ALISON. *The brewing industry: a guide to historical records.* Manchester: Manchester U.P., 1990. See also:

JAMES, R.L.M. 'Brewing records: an inquiry and it's lessons,' *Archives* 7(36), 1966, 215-20.

MATHIAS, PETER. 'Historical records of the brewing industry,' *Archives* 7(33), 1965/6, 2-10.

Much useful research is recorded in the pages of:

Brewery history: the journal of the Brewery History Society. 1972- .

For a topographical history of brewing, with many names of brewers, consult:

BARBER, NORMAN. *A century of British brewers, 1890-1990.* New Ash Green: Brewery History Society, 1994.

A number of substantial directories are available:

The brewers directory and licensed victuallers guide, 1871. Walker & Co., 1871. Alphabetical list.

Duncan's manual of British and foreign brewery companies for 18--. W.W. Duncan & Co., 1889-1902. Annual; title varies. Continued by: *The manual of British and foreign brewery companies.* 1903-47, and by: *The brewery manual.* Attwood & Co., 1948- . Many names of brewing company directors.

The Post Office directory of the brewers and maltsters, and other trades connected therewith, of England, Scotland and Wales, and the principal towns in Ireland. Kelly & Co., 1877.

Brewery manual and who's who in British brewing. Northwood Publications, 1888- . Annual; title varies.

See also Wine and Spirit Trades

Broadcasters

MOSELEY, SYDNEY A. *Who's who in broadcasting: a biographical record of the leading personalities of the microphone.* Sir Isaac Pitman & Sons, 1933.

Radio and television who's who, 1950-51. 2nd ed. Vox Mundi, 1950. 3rd ed., 1954.

Brushmakers

DOUGHTY, K.A. 'Old occupations: brushmaker or tramp?' *Family tree magazine* **9**(5), 1993, 15-17.

Builders

Kelly's directory of the building trades, comprising every trade and profession in any way connected with architecture and building ... Kelly & Co., 1870-1939. Title varies. 22 issues.

The London & provincial builders & building trades directory. W. & T. Piper, 1851. 2nd ed. published as *The Metropolitan & provincial builders and building trades directory.* W. & T. Piper, 1857.

Marchant & Co's metropolitan and provincial builders and building trades directory for 1857, with which is incorporated the engineering, iron and metal trades. Marchant Singer & Co., 1857.

See also Architects and Engineers

Building Society Officers

Building Societies year book, 19--: official handbook of the National Association of Building Societies. Reed & Co., 1927- . The 1928 issue includes a 'Who's who' of building societies.

Businessmen

BASSETT, HERBERT HARRY, ed. *Men of note in finance and commerce, with which is incorporated 'men of office': a biographical business directory.* E. Wilson, 1901.

JEREMY, DAVID J., ed. *Dictionary of business biography: a biographical dictionary of business leaders active in the period 1860-1980.* 5 vols. Butterworth, 1984-6. Includes over 1,000 biographies.

The business world: men and methods of the new Georgian Era: imperial interests, pen sketches, and illustrations. Dod's Publications, 1914. Descriptions of various businesses, many names.

The red book of commerce, or, who's who in business. Grosvenor Press, 1916/17-38?

Business Records

Company archives contain much of interest to the genealogist: staff records, shareholders registers, information on customers etc. For their genealogical value, see:

DAVIS, MAIR. 'Business archives as a source of family history', *Genealogists' magazine* **14**, 1962-4, 332-41.

WATTS, CHRISTOPHER T., & WATTS, MICHAEL J. 'Company records as a source for the family historian', *Genealogists' magazine* **21**(2), 1983, 44-54. General introduction to records of the Registrar of Companies, which give details of directors, shareholders etc.

More detailed guides include:

ARMSTRONG, JOHN, & JONES, STEPHANIE. *Business documents: their origins, sources and uses in historical research.* Mansell, 1987. Of particular interest to genealogists are the chapters on registers of directors, registers of members, diaries, and staff records.

Business Records *continued*

ORBELL, JOHN. *A guide to tracing the history of a business.* Aldershot: Gower, 1987. Although not written for the genealogist, this does suggest many potential leads, and has a good bibliography.

Directories of business records include:

ARMSTRONG, JOHN. *Directory of corporate archives: some corporate members of the Business Archives Council which maintain archive facilities.* Business Archives Council, 1985. List of repositories, with brief notes on holdings.

HISTORICAL MANUSCRIPTS COMMISSION. *Records of British business and industry, 1760-1914: textiles and leather.* Guides to sources for British industry, **8**. H.M.S.O., 1990. Lists papers of over 1,200 firms.

RICHMOND, LESLEY & STOCKFORD, BRIDGET. *Company archives: the survey of the records of 1,000 of the first registered companies in England and Wales.* Gower, 1986. Detailed listing of archives of the oldest surviving limited companies, with notes on company histories. The archives listed include many staff records of genealogical value.

RICHMOND, LESLEY. *Directory of corporate archives: some members of the Business Archives Council which maintain archive facilities.* 2nd ed. Business Archives Council, 1987.

Many histories of individual firms have been published. These sometimes contain pedigrees of the founders, and other useful genealogical information. There are two bibliographies worth checking:

GOODALL, FRANCIS. *A bibliography of British business histories.* Aldershot: Gower, 1987.

ZARACH, STEPHANIE. *Debrett's bibliography of business history.* Macmillan: 1986.

Canal Boatmen

CORFIELD, MIKE. 'Migration of canal workers', *Wiltshire Family History Society [journal]* **19**, 1985, 27-30.

HANSON, HARRY. *The canal boatmen, 1760-1914.* Manchester: Manchester U.P., 1975. Useful for its bibliography, which identifies many potential sources of information.

TRINDER, BARRIE. 'Boatpeople from the 17th to 19th centuries', *Genealogists' magazine* **23**(10), 1991, 374-5. Brief discussion of sources.

See also Boatmen

Candlemakers
See Soapmakers

Cannon Founders
See Gunmakers

Carpenters

HARVEY, JOHN H. 'The King's chief carpenters', *Journal of the British Archaeological Association* 3rd series, **11**, 1948, 13-34. List, 11-16th c., with biographical notes.

See also Architects

Carriers

BATES, ALAN. *Directory of stage coach services, 1836.* Newton Abbot: David & Charles, 1969. Modern compilation, identifying many carriers.

TURNBULL,G.L. 'Provincial road carrying in England in the eighteenth century', *Journal of transport history* N.S., **4**, 1978, 17-39. General discussion, with reference to a number of potentially useful sources.

Cartographers
See Surveyors

Carvers
See Architects

Chancery Officials
See Lawyers

Chaplains

The A.C.U. Chaplains directory. Actors Church Union, 1924- . Irregular; title varies. Lists chaplains to theatres, *etc.*

GRAY, DONALD. *Chaplain to Mr.Speaker: the religious life of the House of Commons.* House of Commons library document **19**. H.M.S.O., 1991. Includes list of chaplains from 1660, with biographical notes.

KEALY, ARTHUR G. *Chaplains of the Royal Navy, 1626-1903.* [ ], 1905. List.

LAURENCE, ANNE. *Parliamentary Army chaplains, 1642-1651.* Royal Historical Society studies in history **59**. Woodbridge: Boydell Press, 1990. Includes a biographical dictionary.

TAYLOR, GORDON. *The sea chaplains of the Royal Navy.* Oxford: Oxford Illustrated Press, 1978. Includes lists of chaplains.

Chapmen
PASSMORE, SUE CAMPBELL. 'Chapman or pedlar', *Family tree magazine* 8(2), 1991, 44-5.

Chelsea Pensioners
BECKETT, J.D., ed. *Index to Chelsea out pensioners, 1st-[104th] infantry regiments, 1806-1838.* 10 fiche. Manchester: Manchester & Lancashire Family History Society, 1990. Also referred to as the *Soldiers Index.*
'The Chelsea pensioners: victims of bureaucracy', *Family tree magazine* 4(9), 1988, 12-13. 19th c. emigrants to Canada; for a list, see also: JONASSON, ERIC. 'The Chelsea pensioners of 1848-50', *Family tree magazine* 5(8), 1989, 26-7.

Chemists
FINDLAY, ALEXANDER, & MILLS, WILLIAM HOBSON, eds. *British chemists.* Chemical Society, 1947. Biographies of 16 prominent chemists.
INSTITUTE OF CHEMISTY OF GREAT BRITAIN AND IRELAND. *A list of official appointments.* The Institute, 1906- . Issued irregularly.
INSTITUTE OF CHEMISTRY OF GREAT BRITAIN AND IRELAND. *Register of fellows, associates and students.* The Institute, 1907- . Title varies; previously published with the Institute's *Proceedings.* Became the ROYAL INSTITUTE OF CHEMISTRY ... with the 1948 issue.
Kelly's directory of chemists and druggists. Kelly & Co., 1869-1916. 13 issues. Title varies.
MOORE, TOM SIDNEY, & PHILIP, JAMES CHARLES. *The Chemical Society, 1841-1941: a historical review.* Chemical Society, 1947. Includes various lists of officers, fellows, medallists, *etc.*
MORRIS, PETER J.T., & RUSSELL, COLIN A. *Archives of the British chemical industry, 1750-1914: a handlist.* Monograph 6. Stanford in the Vale: British Society for the History of Science, 1988. Primarily lists the archives of firms, which often include personnel records.
VICKERS, RAY. 'Old occupations: chemists: the chemical industry to 1914', *Family tree magazine* 9(7), 1993, 27-8.

Chiropractors
See Naturopaths

Chivalric Orders
SIMMONDS, PETER LUND. *The British roll of honour: a descriptive account of the recognised orders of chivalry in various countries, and their insignia, also detailed lists of the British subjects (now living) who have been enrolled in these orders.* Dean & Son, 1887.

Circus Performers
GODDARD, JULIE. 'Lord George Sanger and other circus families', *Family tree magazine* 10(10), 1994, 11.
'Sanger's Circus: 1881 Census', *Family tree magazine* 10(12), 1994, 5. Census list of circus employees.
TOOLE STOTT, RAYMOND. *A bibliography of books on the circus in English from 1773 to 1964.* Derby: Harpur, 1964.
TURNER, J.M. 'Circus family histories', *Family tree magazine* 4(7), 1988, 8. General introduction by the librarian of the Circus Families Association of Great Britain.

Civil Engineers
CHRIMES, MICHAEL. 'The Institution of Civil Engineers' library and archives: a brief introduction', *Construction history: journal of the Construction History Society* 5, 1989, 59-65.
INSTITUTION OF CIVIL ENGINEERS. *Charter bye-laws and list of members of the institution of civil engineers.* The Institution, 1867-1914. Bi-annual. The *List of members ...* was also sometimes published seperately, and has continued publication annually to date.

Civil Servants
There are many works on civil servants. General works are arranged chronologically; this is followed by a departmental listing.
KINNEY, ARTHUR F. *Titled Elizabethans: a directory of Elizabethan state and church officers and knights, with peers of England, Scotland and Ireland, 1558-1603.* Hamden, Connecticut: Arkon Books, 1973
FREEMAN, JESSICA. 'Tudor civil servants: official and semi-official sources in print', *Genealogists' magazine* 22, 1986, 16-17 & 57-9. Discussion based on a case study of the Agard family.

Civil Servants *continued*

PALGRAVE, FRANCIS. 'Calender of specification and surrender rolls', *Sixth report of the Deputy Keeper of the Public Records* 1845, appendix II, 116-203; *Seventh report ...,* 1846, appendix II, 101-87; *Eighth report ...* 1847, appendix II, 82-134. Lists surrenders of crown offices and applications for patents, 1712-1837. No index.

A new and complete list of officers, civil and military, in Great Britain ... Abel Roger & Robert Gosling, 1714. Early list of civil servants.

The court and city register for the year ..., containing I: An almanack for the current year. II: A new and current list of Parliament. III: The court register. IV: Lists of the Army & Navy. T. Cooper, et al., 1743-1814. Title and publisher varies. Includes full lists of office holders, including the armed forces. For full details of the many editions, with locations, see:

MATTHEWS, ALIZON M. 'Bibliographical aids to records, IX: editions of *The court and city register,* 1742-1813', *Bulletin of the Institute of Historical Research* 19, 1942-3, 9-12.

The royal kalender, or, complete and current annual register ... J. Debrett, 1767-1893. Annual; lists the holders of political, public, and court offices.

British Imperial Calendar and civil service list. H.M.S.O., 1809- . Became *Civil Service yearbook* from 1974.

A return of the number of persons on the redundant lists of the public departments at the commencement of the year 1855, the number that have re-entered the public service during the year, the number that have been added during the year, and the number that have remained on the list at the close of the year 1855. House of Commons Parliamentary paper, 1856, **XXXVIII**, 483-577. Many names.

An account of all allowances or compensations granted as retired allowances or superannuations in all public offices or departments, which remained payable on the 1st of January 1859 ... House of Commons Parliamentary papers, 1860, **XL**, 533-81. Identifies many retired civil servants.

The Civil Service yearbook and official calendar. Sheppard & Co., 1873-1917.

The Civil Service directory 1889, containing a list of all the public departments, the officials doing duty therein, and a detailed statement of their services. W.H.Allen & Co., 1889. 1890 issue also seen.

HAYDN, JOSEPH. *The book of dignities, containing lists of the official personages of the British Empire ... from the earliest periods to the present time ...* 3rd. ed. W.H.Allen & Co., 1894. Reprinted: Bath: Firecrest Publishing, 1969. Lists innumerable public officers.

Board of Trade

SAINTY, J.C. *Officials of the Boards of Trade, 1660-1870.* Office-holders in modern Britain, 3. Athlone Press, 1974.

COLLINGE, J.M. *Officials of royal commissions of inquiry, 1815-1870.* Office holders in modern Britain, 9. Institute of Historical Research, 1984.

Home Ofice

SAINTY, J.C. *Home Office officials, 1782-1870.* Office-holders in modern Britain, 5. Athlone Press, 1975.

Ministry of Munitions

Ministry of Munitions of war: list of staff and distribution of duties. [The Ministry], 1918.

Secretaries of State

SAINTY, J.C. *Officials of the Secretaries of State, 1660-1782.* Office-holders in modern Britain, 2. Athlone Press, 1973.

Treasury

SAINTY, J.C. *Treasury officials, 1660-1870.* Office-holders in modern Britain, 1. Athlone Press, 1972.

See also Clerks of the Closet, Colonial Officials, Exchequer Officials, Household Officials, Inland Revenue Officers, and Naval Administrators.

Clayworkers

The directory of clayworkers. British Clayworkers Offices, 1901-4. 2 issues.

Clergy

There is an enormous amount of literature devoted to the history of the clergy, and many books are available which could be of use to genealogists. Only a small selection is listed here. A few other works are listed below under the headings 'Monks and religious orders', and 'Students and scholars (Roman Catholic)'. The general works on the Church of England listed in Raymond's *English Genealogy: a bibliography,* section 14a, are important for tracing clergy, and should be consulted; the list is not repeated here. The county volumes of *British genealogical bibliographies* (see back cover) identify many lists of incumbents for particular parishes. The compilation of such lists is discussed, and many useful hints are given, in:

BRINKWORTH, E.R.C. 'The records of the clergy', *Amateur historian* 2(3), 1954-5, 82-6.

The most important list of incumbents is that compiled by Le Neve for diocesan officials. This was originally published in 1784, but is currently being issued in a much revised edition. Volumes published to date include:

LE NEVE, JOHN. *Fasti ecclesiae Anglicanae, 1066-1300,* comp. Diana E. Greenway. Athlone Press, 1968- . Contents: v.1. St.Pauls, London. v.2. Monastic Cathedrals. v.3. Lincoln.

LE NEVE, JOHN. *Fasti ecclesiase Anglicanae, 1300-1541.* 12 vols. Athlone Press. 1962-7, Contents: v.1. Lincoln Diocese, comp. H.P.F. King. v.2. Hereford Diocese, comp. Joyce M. Horn. v.3. Salisbury Diocese, comp. Joyce M. Horn. v.4. Monastic Cathedrals (Southern Province), comp. B. Jones. v.5. St.Pauls, London, comp. Joyce M. Horn. v.6. Chichester Diocese, comp. Joyce M. Horn. v.8. Bath and Wells Diocese, comp. Joyce M. Horn. v.9. Exeter Diocese, comp. Joyce M. Horn. v.10. Coventry & Lichfield Diocese, comp. B. Jones. v.11. The Welsh Dioceses (Bangor, Llandaff, St. Asaph, St. Davids), comp. B Jones. v.12. Introduction, errata and index, comp. Joyce M. Horn.

LE NEVE, JOHN. *Fasti ecclesiae Anglicanae, 1541-1857.* Athlone Press, 1969- . Contents: v.1. St. Pauls, London, comp. Joyce M. Horn. v.2. Chichester Diocese, comp. Joyce M. Horn. v.3. Canterbury, Rochester and Winchester Dioceses, comp. Joyce M. Horn. v.4. York Diocese, comp. Joyce M. Horn & David M. Smith. v.5. Bath and Wells Diocese, comp. Joyce M. Horn & Derrick Sherwin Bailey. v.6. Salisbury Diocese, comp. Joyce M. Horn.

Many other clergy lists and other works useful for identifying churchmen are available. The following works are arranged in rough chronological order:

DAVIS, VIRGINIA. 'Medieval English clergy database', *History and computing* **2**, 1990, 75-87. Description of a project to computerise medieval ordination lists.

LLOYD, A.H. 'Notes on Cambridge clerks petitioning for benefices, 1370-1399', *Bulletin of the Institute of Historical Research* **20**, 1943-5, 75-96 & 192-211. Based on records in the Vatican Archives; includes brief biographical details of clergy in many dioceses.

SOMERVILLE, ROBERT. 'Duchy of Lancaster presentations, 1399-1485', *Bulletin of the Institute of Historical Research* **18**, 1941, 52-76. Lists clergy presented to benefices in many counties.

GARRETT, CHRISTINA HALLOWELL. *Marian exiles: a study in the origin of Elizabethan puritanism.* Cambridge: C.U.P., 1938. Biographical dictionary of exiles, 1553-9.

BROOK, BENJAMIN. *The lives of the puritans, containing a biographical account of those divines who distinguished themselves in the cause of religious liberty from the Reformation under Queen Elizabeth to the Act of Uniformity in 1662.* J. Black, 1813.

GEE, HENRY. *The Elizabethan clergy and the settlement of religion, 1558-1564.* Oxford: Clarendon Press, 1898. Includes various lists of clergy.

PEEL, ALBERT, ed. *The seconde parte of a register, being a calendar of manuscripts under that title intended for publication by the Puritans about 1593 ...* Cambridge: C.U.P., 1915. Lists clergy for many dioceses, with the opinions of puritans on their work.

MATTHEWS, A.G. *Walker revised, being a revision of John Walker's 'sufferings of the clergy during the Grand Rebellion, 1642-60'.* Oxford: Clarendon Press, 1948. A full name index is provided separately: SURMAN, CHARLES E. *A.G. Matthews' 'Walker revised': supplementary index of intruders and others.* Occasional paper 2. Dr Williams Library, 1956.

MATTHEWS, A.G. *Calamy revised: being a revision of Edmund Calamy's Account of the ministers and others ejected and silenced, 1660-2.* Oxford: Clarendon Press, 1934. Biographical dictionary listing 1,760 clergy.

Clergy *continued*

WATSON, R.T. 'Presentations on the Patent Rolls, Charles II', *Forty-sixth annual report of the Deputy Keeper of the Public Records*, 1885, appendix 1, 18-26.

OVERTON, J.H. *The nonjurors, their lives, principals and writings.* Smith, Elder & Co., 1902. Includes list of clergy unwilling to take the oath of allegiance to William and Mary after the Glorious Revolution, 1688.

FOTHERGILL, GERALD. *A list of emigrant ministers to America, 1690-1811.* Elliott Stock, 1904. For additions, see *New England historical and genealogical register* **59**, 1905, 218-9.

FOSTER, JOSEPH. *Index ecclesiasticus, or alphabetical list of all ecclesiastical dignitaries in England and Wales since the Reformation, containing 150,000 hitherto unpublished entries from the bishops certificates of institutions to livings etc., now deposited in the Public Record Office, and including those names which appear in Le Neve's 'Fasti'.* Oxford: Parker & Co., 1890. This work was never completed. Only the portion covering the years 1800-40, listing c.6,000 clergy, was actually published.

HISTORICAL MANUSCRIPTS COMMISSION. *Papers of British churchmen, 1780-1940.* Guides to sources for British history, **6**. H.M.S.O., 1987. Lists papers of over 700 churchmen, of various denominations.

The clerical guide, or ecclesiastical directory, containing a complete register of the prelates and other dignitaries of the church, a list of all the benefices in England and Wales, arranged alphabetically in their several counties, dioceses, archdeaconries, &c., the names of their respective incumbents, the population of the parishes, value of the livings, names of the pastors, &c., &c., ... 4th edition. F.C.& J. Rivington, 1817-36. Title varies.

The clergy list for 1846, containing alphabetical list of the clergy, list of the clergy of the Scottish Episcopal church ... C. Cox, 1846-99. Annual; publisher varies.

Crockford's clerical directory. Church House Publishing, *et al.,* 1858- . Includes brief biographical notes on all Church of England clergymen. The standard source for the 20th century.

ROYAL, ARTHUR. 'Parsons galore', *Family tree magazine* **8**(12), 1992, 28-9. Discussion of *Crockfords Clerical dictionary.*

LONDON COLLEGE OF DIVINITY. *List of clergy ordained prior to 1889, who are still in union with the college.* Gilbert Rivington, [1890?] Anglican clergy throughout the country.

WALLER, C.H. *The London College of Divinity, 1863-1897: governing body, tutors, lecturers, and clergy.* Elliot Stock, 1898.

The clergy directory and parish guide: an alphabetical list of the clergy of the Church of England ... Thomas Bosworth, 1873-1930. Annual.

Church of England yearbook: the official yearbook of the General Synod of the Church of England. Church Information Office, 1882- . Annual; includes who's who of leading churchmen.

BOSWORTH, THOMAS. *Bosworth's clerical guide and ecclesiastical directory.* 3 vols. T.Bosworth & Co., Hamilton Adams & Co., 1886-8.

The church directory and almanack ... James Nisbet & Co., 1901-47. Annual. Title varies. Includes clergy list.

The ritualistic clergy list: a guide for patrons & others to certain of the clergy of the Church of England, being a list of over 9000 clergymen who are helping the Romeward movement in the national church ... 4th ed. Church Association, 1908.

USSHER, RICHARD. *Roll of the sons & daughters of the Anglican Church clergy throughout the world, and of the naval & military chaplains of the same, who gave their lives in the great war, 1914-1918.* English Crafts and Monumental Society, [1925?]

See also Chaplains.

Nonconformists

There are also many sources for identifying nonconformist clergy. For general discussions of nonconformist records, see the works listed in Raymond's *English Genealogy: a bibliography* section 14B. The essential guides are:

PALGRAVE-MOORE, T.R. *Understanding the history and records of nonconformity.* Norwich: Elvery Dowers, 1987.

STEEL, D.J. *Sources for nonconformist genealogy and family history.* National index of parish registers, **2**. Society of Genealogists, 1973.

Baptists

The Baptist manual ... Houlstone & Stoneman, 1845-59. Continued by *The Baptist handbook.* Baptist Union of Great Britain & Ireland, 1860- . Lists ministers, etc.

LANGLEY, ARTHUR S. 'Baptist ministers in England about 1750 A.D.', *Transactions of the Baptist Historical Society* **6**, 1918-19, 138-62. List.

WHITLEY, W.T. *A Baptist bibliography: being a register of the chief materials for Baptist history, whether in manuscript or print, preserved in Great Britain, Ireland and the colonies.* 2 vols. Kingsgate Press, 1916-22. v.1. 1526-1776. v.2. 1777-1837, & addenda. Includes information on registers, and many biographical notes.

WHITLEY, W.T., ed. *Minutes of the General Assembly of the General Baptist Churches in England, with kindred records.* Kingsgate Press for the Baptist Historical Society, 1909-10. v.1. 1654-1728. v.2. 1731-1811. Gives many names of ministers, etc.

Congregationalists

GORDON, ALEXANDER. *Freedom after ejection: a review (1690-1692) of Presbyterian and Congregational nonconformity in England and Wales.* Manchester: Manchester U.P., 1917. Includes biographical notes on 760 ministers.

PEEL, ALBERT. *The Congregational two hundred, 1530-1948.* Independent Press, 1948. Brief biographies.

YULE, GEORGE. *The Independents in the English civil war.* Cambridge: C.U.P., 1958. Includes a list of congregational ministers, 1640-60.

The Congregational year book. Nottingham: Congregational Federation, 1846-1972. Publisher varies. Includes biographical information on clergy, etc.

Who's who in Congregationalism: an authoritative reference work and guide to the careers of ministers and lay officials of the congregational churches. Shaw, 1934.

Huguenots

MANCHÉE, W.H. 'Huguenot clergy list, 1548-1916', *Proceedings of the Huguenot Society of London* **11**, 1915-17, 263-92. See also 387-99. Supplemented by:

MINET, S. 'Huguenot ministers in Great Britain', *Proceedings of the Huguenot Society of London* **19**(4), 1956, 170-87.

Methodists

GARLICK, KENNETH B. *Mr Wesley's preachers: an alphabetical arrangement of Wesleyan Methodist preachers and missionaries, and the stations to which they were appointed, 1739-1818.* Pinhorns, for the World Methodist Historical Society (British Section), 1977.

HALL, JOSEPH. *Hall's circuits and ministers: an alphabetical list of the circuits of Great Britain, with the names of the ministers stationed in each circuit from 1765 to [19--].* Rev. ed. Methodist Publishing House, 1914. Supplements, 1914 and 1925.

HALL, JOSEPH. *Memorials of Wesleyan Methodist ministers, or, the yearly death roll from 1777 to 1840 ...* Haughton & Co., 1876.

JACKSON, THOMAS, ed. *The lives of early Methodist preachers, chiefly written by themselves.* 6 vols. 4th ed. Wesleyan Conference Offices, 1871-2.

STEVENSON, G.J. *Methodist worthies: characteristic sketches of Methodist preachers of the several denominations, with historical sketch of each denomination.* 6 vols. Thomas C. Jack, 1884-8.

LEARY, WILLIAM. *Ministers and circuits in the Primitive Methodist Church: being an alphabetically arranged directory of all Primitive Methodist ministers and the circuits they served, from 1819 to the date of death, or, if still living, to the date of superannuation.* Loughborough: Teamprint, in association with the World Methodist Historical Society, 1990.

MICHELL, WILLIAM JOHN. *Brief biographical sketches of Bible Christian ministers and laymen.* 2 vols. Jersey: Beresford Press, 1905-6.

BECKERLEGGE, OLIVER A. *United Methodist ministers and their circuits, being an arrangement in alphabetical order of the stations of ministers of the Methodist New Connexion, Bible Christians, Arminian Methodists, Protestant Methodists, Wesleyan Methodist Association, Wesleyan Reformers, United Methodist Free Churches, and the United Methodist Church, 1797-1932.* Epworth Press, 1968.

25

Clergy, Methodists *continued*

METHODIST CHURCH. *Ministers and probationers of the Methodist church ...* Methodist Publishing House, 1932- . Irregular.

Who's who in Methodism 1933: an encyclopaedia of the personnel and departments, ministerial and lay in the united church of Methodism. Methodist Times and Leader, 1933.

Garlick's methodist registry, 1983. Edsall of London, 1983. Biographical dictionary of living ministers, plus lists of various officials from the beginning.

Presbyterians

CREASEY, JOHN. *Index to the John Evans list of dissenting congregations and ministers, 1715-1729 in Dr. Williams' Library.* Dr. Williams Trust, 1964. Predominantly lists Presbyterian clergy.

GORDON, ALEXANDER. *Freedom after ejection: a review (1690-1692) of Presbyterian and Congregational nonconformity in England and Wales.* Manchester: Manchester University Press, 1917. The so-called 'index' of this work in fact includes a biographical dictionary of ministers.

See also Congregationalists

Roman Catholics

Printed sources for tracing Roman Catholics clergy are numerous. The best introductions to this literature are two general guides to Roman Catholic genealogy:

STEEL, D.J. & SAMUEL, E.R. *Sources for Roman Catholic and Jewish genealogy and family history.* National index of parish registers, **3**. Phillimore, for the Society of Genealogists, 1974.

WILLIAMS, J.A. *Recusant history: sources for recusant history (1559 to 1791) in English official archives.* Catholic Record Society, 1983.

Reference should also be made to the other works listed in section 14J of Raymond's *English genealogy: a bibliography.*

Many useful sources are published in:

Catholic Record Society publications. The Society, 1905- .

Other useful works include:

ANSTRUTHER, G. *The seminary priests: a dictionary of the secular clergy of England and Wales, 1558-1850.* 4 vols. Ware: St Edmunds College, Great Wakering: Mayhew-McCrimmon, 1969- .

BELLENGER, DOMINIC AIDAN. *English and Welsh priests 1558-1800: a working list.* Bath: Downside Abbey, 1984.

BELLENGER, DOMINIC AIDAN. *The French exiled clergy in the British Isles after 1789: an historical introduction and working list.* Bath: Downside Abbey, 1986. Includes 120 page list.

The Catholic directory of England and Wales. Manchester: Burns & Oates, 1838- . Annual. Title and publisher varies. Lists clergy.

GILLOW, JOSEPH. *A literary and biographical history, or bibliographical dictionary of English Catholics from the breach with Rome, in 1534, to the present time.* 5 vols. Burns & Oates, 1885-1902. Includes biographies of many priests.

KIRK, JOHN. *Biographies of English Catholics in the eighteenth century,* ed. John Hungerford Pollen & Edwin Burton. Burns & Oates, 1909. Use with caution.

MACRAY, W.D. 'Necrology of Roman Catholic clergy, 1670-1678', *Palatine note-book* **3**, 1883, 101-4. See also 173-5. Lists clergy deaths.

STANFIELD, RAYMUND. 'Obituaries of secular priests, 1722-1783, from the archives of the Old Brotherhood, formerly the Old Chapter of England', *Publications of the Catholic Record Society* **12**, 1913, 1-15.

The Catholic directory and annual register for the year 18--. James Smith, 1838- . Title and publisher vary; includes extensive lists of clergy, *etc.*

The Catholic who's who & yearbook. Burns & Oates, 1908-42. *Title varies.*

See also Monks and Religious Orders, and Students and Scholars (Roman Catholic)

Unitarians

The Essex Hall directory of ministers and congregations of Great Britain and Ireland. British and Foreign Unitarian Association, 1904-11. Continued as *Directory of Unitarian Ministers and congregations.* British & Foreign Unitarian Association, 1911- .

The Essex Hall yearbook for 18--. British and Foreign Unitarian Society, 1894-1928. Continued by *Yearbook of the General Assembly of Unitarian and Free Christian Churches for 19--.* Essex Hall, 1929- . Title varies; includes names of Unitarian ministers and lay officers.

Clerks of the Closet
BICKERSTETH, JOHN, & DUNNING, R.W. *Clerks of the closet in the royal household: five hundred years of service to the crown.* Stroud: Alan Sutton, 1991. Includes full list of clerks 1437-1989; also list of sources.

Clerks of the Counties
STEPHENS, EDGAR, SIR. *The clerks of the counties, 1360-1960.* Newport: Society of the Clerk of the Peace of Counties, and of Clerks of County Councils, 1961. List with biographical notes.

Clockmakers
AKED, CHARLES K. *Complete list of English horological patents up to 1853.* Ashford: Brant Wright Associates, 1975. List with notes on patents, and dates.

BAILLIE, G.H. *Watchmakers and clockmakers of the world.* 3rd ed. N.A.G. Press. 1951. Reprinted as vol. 1, 1976, to accompany the 1st edition of LOOMES, BRIAN E. *Watchmakers and clockmakers of the world,* vol. 2. 2nd ed. Colchester: N.A.G. Press, 1989. These two volumes list 70,000 makers, and are particularly detailed for the U.K.

BRITTEN, F.J. *Britten's old clocks and watches and their makers: a history of styles in clocks and watches and their mechanisms,* ed. G.H. Baillie, Courtenay Ilbert, & Cecil Clutton. 9th ed. Bloomsbury Books, 1986. Includes extensive list of makers.

Kelly's directory of the watch, clock and jewellery trades. Kelly & Co., 1872-1937. Title varies; 16 issues.

LOOMES, BRIAN. *The early clockmakers of Great Britain.* N.A.G. Press, 1981. Biographical dictionary of c.5,000 clockmakers.

Clogmakers
PASSMORE, SUE. 'Old occupations: Clogmakers,' *Family tree magazine* 8(3), 1992, 4-5.

Clothiers
RAMSAY, G.D. 'The distribution of the cloth industry in 1561-2', *English historical review* 57, 1942, 361-9. Includes list of country clothiers fined for defective cloth at Blackwell Hall, London.

ZELL, MICHAEL L. 'The Exchequer lists of provincial clothmakers fined in London during the sixteenth century', *Bulletin of the Institute of Historical Research* 54, 1981, 129-30. General discussion of a little-known source.

Limitation of Supplies (Cloth and Apparel) Order, 1941. List of persons whose names were on 15th October 1941 entered in the cloth and apparel register ... H.M.S.O., 1942.

Coachmen
MAURIN, MARGARET. 'Coaches and coachmen', *Family tree magazine* 11(6), 1995, 3-5.

YOUNG, ROSA. 'Following the stagecoaches', *Local historian* 14(6), 1981, 341-6. Discussion of sources.

Coal Merchants
The coal trades' directory, comprising all the important trades and professions connected with coal and iron throughout England, Scotland and Wales, with an Irish and foriegn appendix of manufacturers and merchants. Eyre Bros., 1877.

Coiners
RAYNER, P.A. *The designers and engravers of the English milled coinage, 1662-1953.* B.A. Seaby. 1954.

Records of the Royal Mint, 1446-20th c. (MINT 1-29). List & Index Society, **234**. 1989. Lists staff records, amongst much else, held at the Public Record Office.

Colliers
BENSON, JOHN, NEVILLE, ROBERT G., & THOMPSON, CHARLES H. *Bibliography of the British coal industry: secondary literature, parliamentary and departmental papers, mineral maps and plans and a guide to the sources.* Oxford: O.U.P., for the National Coal Board, 1981. The guide to primary source material may yield useful clues.

Colliers *continued*

DUCKHAM, BARON. 'A colliery history', *Local historian* **8**, 1968-9, 272-81. Discussion of research in mining history, including a bibliography, which may prove useful.

Reports of ... Inspectors of Coal Mines. House of Commons papers. H.M.S.O., 1851- . Published annually, these frequently give the names of miners involved in accidents, and the names of mine owners. See the list of reports in COCKTON, PETER. *Subject catalogue of the House of Commons papers, 1801-1900,* v.2., 109-10.

See also Coal Merchants

Colonial Officials

The Colonial Office list. H.M.S.O., 1862-1966. Annual; title varies.

HISTORICAL MANUSCRIPTS COMMISSION. *Private papers of British colonial governors.* Guides to sources of British history, 5. H.M.S.O., 1986. Lists papers of 353 governors.

HENIGE, DAVID. *Colonial governors from the fifteenth century to the present: a comprehensive list.* Madison: University of Wisconsin Press, 1970. Includes governors of all the colonial powers, not just Great Britain.

KIRK-GREENE, A.H.M. *A biographical dictionary of the British colonial governor, vol. 1: Africa.* Harvester Press, 1980. Includes a useful discussion of the sources used, with detailed notes on each governor.

KIRK-GREENE, A.H.M. *A biographical dictionary of the British Colonial Service, 1939-1966.* Hans Zell, 1991.

SAINTY, J.C. *Colonial Office officials: officials of the Secretary of State for War, 1794-1801, of the Secretary of State for War and Colonies, 1801-54, and of the Secretary of State for Colonies, 1854-70.* Office-holders in modern Britain, **6**. Institute of Historical Research, 1976.

Colonialists

SIMPSON, DONALD H. *Biography catalogue of the library of the Royal Commonwealth Society.* Royal Commonwealth Society, 1961. Lists many biographies of colonialists.

Combmakers

BOWERS, RON. *Combs, combmaking and the Combmakers Company.* Honiton: The author, 1987. Gives over 1000 names of combmakers throughout the British Isles.

WATTS, ROBERT H. 'Old occupations: the combmaker,' *Family tree magazine* **10**(12), 1994, 54-5.

Company archives

See Business Records

Company Secretaries

See Directors (Company)

Composers

See Musicians

Convicts

See Criminals

Cookery Teachers

The Epicure directory of schools and teachers of cookery and domestic subjects. The Epicure, 1899.

Cooperative Workers and Members

GARRATT, ROY. 'The Cooperative Union Library,' *Manchester Region history review* **5**(1), 1991, 35-9.

LAZELL, DAVID. 'A check at the Co-op', *Family tree magazine* **9**(8), 1993, 44-5.

Coroners

HUNNISETT, R.F. *The medieval coroner.* Cambridge: C.U.P., 1961. General discussion.

GIBSON, JEREMY,& ROGERS, COLIN. *Coroners' records in England and Wales.* Birmingham: Federation of Family History Societies, 1989.

Councillors

The municipal corporation directory 1866 ... Longmans, Green and Co., 1866. Includes names of mayors, magistrates, aldermen, councillors, and various other officers.

The county councillor's directory, containing a list of the aldermen and councillors, with addresses, for all counties and county boroughs, under the act of 1888. Contract Journal Co., [1889-92]. 2 issues. Includes a list of members of the Incorporated Association of Municipal and County Engineers.

Municipal directory for the United Kingdom.
Sanitary Publishing Co., 1895. Lists chairmen
and chief officers.

Who's who in local government. Municipal
Journal, 1931. Biographical dictionary of
councillors and officers.

Craftsmen

HARVEY, JOHN. 'Genealogical problems of
medieval craftsmen', *Genealogists' magazine*
11, 1951, 45-61. Includes list of medieval
architects and masons.

COYSH, ARTHUR WILFRED. *The antique buyers
dictionary of names.* Rev. ed. Newton Abbot:
David and Charles, 1972. Biographical notes
on the makers of antiques.

Cricketers

BAILEY, PHILIP, THORN, PHILIP, & WYNNE-
THOMAS, PETER. *Who's who of cricketers: a
complete who's who of all cricketers who
have played first class cricket in England,
with full career records.* Feltham: Newnes
Books, 1984.

BROOKE, ROBERT. *The Collins who's who of
English first-class cricket, 1945-1984.* Willow
Books, 1985.

CAPLE, S.CANYNGE. *The cricketer's who's who.*
5 pts. Hunstanton: Cricket Book Society,
1946-8. Incomplete; reached 'Every' before
cessation.

DOREY, H.V. *Cricket who's who: the blue book
of cricket.* Cricket Publishing, 1909-13.
Annual. Publisher varies.

FRINDALL, BILL. *The Kaye book of cricket
records.* Kaye & Ward, 1968. Lists numerous
cricketers and their scores.

GREEN, BENNY. *The Wisden book of
obituaries: obituaries from Wisden cricketer's
almanack, 1892-1985.* Queen Anne Press,
1986. Of 8,614 obituaries in *Wisdens,* about
one fifth - mainly those who died 1914-18 -
have been omitted from this work.

MARCH, RUSSELL. *The cricketers of Vanity
Fair.* Exeter: Webb & Bower, 1982. Includes
biographies of famous cricketers.

MARTIN-JENKINS, CHRISTOPHER. *The complete
who's who of test cricketers.* Rev. ed. Queen
Anne Press, 1987.

PADWICK, E.W. *A bibliography of cricket.* 2nd
ed. Library Association, 1984. Lists numerous
collective and individual biographies.

Continued by: ELEY, STEPHEN, &
GRIFFITHS, PETER. *Padwick's bibliography
of cricket.* Library Association, 1991.
Covers publications of 1980-89.

WAGHORN, HENRY THOMAS. *The dawn of
cricket,* ed. Lord Harris. R. Tomsett & Co.,
for the Marylebone Cricket Club, 1906.
Includes lists of numerous teams.

WEBBER, ROY. *Test match captains, 1876-1939.*
Hunstanton: Cricket Book Society, 1946.
List only.

WEBBER, ROY. *Who's who in world cricket.*
Hodder & Stoughton, 1952.

Criminals

The essential guide to sources for
researching criminals is:

HAWKINGS, DAVID. *Criminal ancestors: a
guide to historical criminal records in
England and Wales.* Stroud: Alan Sutton,
1992. Very detailed and extensive.

Written for Australians, but also of use to a
wider audience, is:

REAKES, JANET. *How to trace your convict
ancestors: their lives, times and records.*
Sydney: Hale & Iremonger, 1987.

A number of brief journal articles are
available:

CHAMBERS, JILL. 'Indexers and their indexes:
machine breakers and convicts', *Family
tree magazine* **9**(11), 1993, 23.

HAWKINGS, DAVID. 'Criminal ancestors in
England and Wales', *Family tree magazine*
8(5), 1992, 43-4.

PARRY, COLIN J. 'Prisons and census returns',
Genealogists' magazine **20**(4), 1980, 124-5.
Brief note.

PARRY, COLIN J. 'Missing from home, pt.2:
Prisons', *Family tree magazine* **3**(7), 1987,
27-8. Discussion of 1851 census, including
extracts.

SWIFT, ROGER. 'Sources and methods for the
study of urban criminals in the early
nineteenth century', *Local historian* **16**(5),
1985, 289-97. Includes information on
sources of potential genealogical value.

WOOD, TOM. 'Criminals and convicts', *Family
tree magazine* **7**(12), 1991, 15-16; **8**(1), 1991,
15-16.

For a guide to the literature on the history
of crime, see:

Criminals *continued*

KNAFLA, L.A. 'Crime and criminal justice: a critical bibliography', in COCKBURN, J.S., ed. *Crime in England, 1550-1800.* Methuen, 1977, 270-98.

Other works include:

BELLAMY, J.G. 'The Coteral gang: an anatomy of a band of fourteenth-century criminals,' *English historical review* **79**, 1964, 698-717. Anatomy of a gang operating throughout the north of England.

HAYWARD, ARTHUR L., ed. *Lives of the most remarkable criminals who have been condemned and executed for murder, the highway, housebreaking, street robberies, coining, or other offences.* George Routledge & Sons, 1927. Originally published 1735; covers the period 1726-35.

KNAPP, ANDREW. *The Newgate calendar, or malefactore's bloody register, containing genuine and circumstantial narrative of the lives and transactions, various exploits, and dying speeches of the most notorious criminals of both sexes who suffered death punishment in Gt. Britain and Ireland ...* New ed. Laurie, 1933. There are many editions of this book, which includes biographies of numerous criminals.

PRIESTLY, PHILIP. *Victorian prison lives: English prison biography, 1830-1914.* Methuen, 1985.

SMITH, ALEXANDER. *A complete history of the lives and robberies of the most notorious highwaymen, footpads, shoplifts & cheats of both sexes ...,* ed. Arthur L. Hayward. 5th ed. Routledge & Sons, 1926. Originally published 1719.

Customs and Excise Officers

HOWARTH, J. 'John Siddall: excise officer', *Family tree magazine* **5**(1), 1988, 32-3. Includes much information on the Excise service.

JARVIS, RUPERT C. 'The records of the customs and excise services', *Genealogists' magazine* **10**(7), 1948, 219-25. Primarily a discussion of staff records.

JARVIS, RUPERT C. 'The local archives of H.M. Customs,' *Society of Local Archivists bulletin* **9**, 1952, 1-14. Discussion of records relating to customs officers, ship owners, *etc.*

LODEY, JOY. 'Was your ancestor a customs officer?' *Family tree magazine* **5**(10), 1989, 3-5.

See also Smugglers

Cycle Tradesmen

PORTER, F. *Postal directory of the cycle trades of Great Britain and Ireland.* Liverpool: Rockliff Bros., 1896.

Dancers

{See Actors

Dentists

HILLAM, CHRISTINE. *Brass plate and brazen impudence: dental practice in the provinces 1755-1855.* Liverpool: Liverpool University Press, 1991. Includes list of 2000 provincial dentists.

The dentists register. General Council of Medical Education & Registration, et al., 1879- . Published under Act of Parliament.

The dental annual and directory: a yearbook of dental surgery ... Bailliere Tindall and Cox, 1903-6. 4 issues.

The dental directory containing the names and addresses of all registered dental practitioners, with description and date of qualification, practicing in the United Kingdom, the colonies, abroad, compiled from official sources. John Bale, Sons and Danielsson, 1909-15.

The dental surgeons directory, 1925, comprising graduates and licentiates in dental surgery, local lists, schools of dental surgery, dental hospitals and dental societies. J.and A. Churchill, 1925. Previously part of the *Medical directory.* Gives addresses and positions.

Diplomats

BELL, GARY M. *A handlist of British diplomatic representatives,1509-1688.* Guides and handbooks **16.** Royal Historical Society, 1990.

BASCHET, M.ARMAND 'Lists of despatches of ambassadors from France to England, Henry VIII - George I, 1509-1714,' *Thirty-ninth annual report of the Deputy Keeper of the Public Records,* 1878, appendix, 573-826.

BASCHET, M. ARMAND. 'Lists of French ambassadors &c., in England, Henry VIII-

Anne, 1509-1714,' *Thirty-seventh annual report of the Deputy Keeper of the Public Records,* 1876, appendix 180-94.

BINDOFF, S.T., SMITH, E.F.MALCOLM, & WEBSTER, E.K. *British diplomatic representatives, 1789-1859.* Camden 3rd series **50.** Royal Historical Society, 1934.

FIRTH, C.H., ed. *Notes on the diplomatic relations of England and France.* Oxford: B.H. Blackwell, 1909. Includes list of diplomatic representatives and agents, 1689-1763.

FIRTH, C.H. *Notes on the diplomatic relations of England with the north of Europe.* Oxford: B.H. Blackwell, 1913. Includes list of diplomats in Denmark, Sweden & Russia, 1689-1762.

FIRTH, C.H. *Notes on the diplomatic relations of England and Germany.* Oxford: B.H. Blackwell, 1907. Includes list of diplomats, 1689-1727.

HORN, D.B. *British diplomatic representatives, 1689-1789.* Camden 3rd series, **46.** Royal Historical Society, 1932. List with brief notes on their overseas appointments.

COLLINGE, J.M. *Foreign Office officials, 1782-1870.* Office-holders in modern Britain, **8.** Institute of Historical Research, 1979.

HISTORICAL MANUSCRIPTS COMMISSION. *Private papers of British diplomats, 1782-1900.* Guides to sources for British history, **4.** H.M.S.O., 1985. Lists papers of 382 diplomats.

The Foreign Office list, 18--, forming a complete diplomatic and consular handbook ... Harrison & Sons, 1852-1965. Title varies; includes 'statement of services', outlining the careers of F.O. officers.

Directors (Company)

The directory of directors. T. Skinner & Co., 1880- . Annual. Alphabetical list of directors with names of their companies.

The directory of secretaries: a directory of the secretaries, actuaries, managers and chief officials of joint stock companies, banks, societies, institutions, etc., having offices within the United Kingdom. Blades East and Blades, 1891.

COWARD, EDWARD. *Coward's directory of secretaries.* F.W.Sullivan, 1896-8. 2 issues. Lists company secretaries.

Directors (Theatrical)
See Actors

Dog Exhibitors
The kennel directory and dog owner's guide. Exhibitor's Supply Association, 1912-13. Lists exhibitors.

Dramatists
See Actors, Musicians, and Poets.

Drovers
PASSMORE, SUE CAMPBELL. 'Old occupations: drovers, *Family tree magazine* **8**(10), 1992, 4-5; **8**(11), 1992, 4-5.

Duchy of Lancaster Officeholders
SOMERVILLE, ROBERT. *History of the Duchy of Lancaster, volume 1: 1265-1603.* Chancellor and Council of the Duchy of Lancaster, 1953. Includes extensive list of office holders throughout England and Wales.

SOMERVILLE, ROBERT. *Office-holders in the Duchy and County of Lancaster from 1603.* Phillimore, 1972.

East India Men (including Indian Army.)
BAXTER, IAN A. *A brief guide to biographical sources.* India Office Library & Records, 1979. The essential guide for tracing East India men.

BULLOCK, HUMPHRY. 'Anglo-Indian family history', *Amateur historian* 1(4), 1953, 117-22. Now out of date, but still worth reading.

DANVERS, FREDERICK CHARLES, et al. *Memorials of old Haileybury College.* Archibald Constable and Company, 1894. Includes biographical notes on students. *etc.,* preparing to serve the East India Company prior to 1857.

FARRINGTON, ANTHONY. *Guide to the records of the India Office Military Department.* India Office Library and Records: guide to Archive Groups, **2.** British Library, 1982.

FARRINGTON, ANTHONY. *The records of the East India College, Haileybury, & other institutions.* India Office Records guide to archive groups J-K. H.M.S.O., 1976. Includes a valuable index to petitions for writerships, 1749-1856, as well as staff lists and notes on other records.

East India Men *continued*

FITZHUGH, T.V.H. 'East India Company ancestry', *Genealogists' magazine* **21**(5), 1984, 150-4. General discussion of records.

FITZHUGH, TERRICK. 'The India Office records as a biographical source', *Family history* **12**(85/6), N.S., **61/2**, 1981, 41-51.

HODSON, V.C.P. 'India Office records: a lecture', *Genealogists' magazine* **6**, 1932-4, 198-208.

HODSON, V.C.P. 'Some families with a long East India connexion', *Genealogists' magazine* **6**, 1932-4, 18-22, 63-6, 103-6, 159-64, 247-53, 294-8 & 355-62. Includes pedigrees of 51 families.

India Office records: sources for family history research. British Library, 1988.

MOIR, MARTIN. *A general guide to the India Office records.* British Library, 1988. Briefly lists many records relating to merchants, seamen, etc., e.g. registers of births, marriages and death, Haileybury records, establishment records, etc.

ROHATGI, PAULINE. *Portraits in the India Office Library and records.* British Library, 1983. Extensive; also includes indexes of painters and sculptors, engravers and lithographers, and photographers.

TAYLOR, NEVILLE C. *Sources for Anglo-Indian genealogy in the library of the Society of Genealogists.* Society of Genealogists, 1990.

BAXTER, I.A. 'Records of the Poplar Pension Fund,' *East London record* **8**, 1985, 30-33. Discusses records of East India Company Pensions, 19th c.

BAXTER, I.A. 'The Poplar Pension Fund,' *Cockney ancestor* **27**, 1985, 14-17.

Lists

Numerous lists of company servants, both civil and military, are available. A number of periodicals attempted to provide regular listings; these were:

A new oriental register and East-India directory ... A.& J.Black, and H.Parry, 1800-1802. 2 issues.

An East-India register and directory for 18--, containing complete lists of the Company's servants, civil,. military and marine ... Cox Son and Baylis, 1803-9. Bi-annual.

CLARK, F. *The East India register and army list for 18--.* Wm.H.Allen & Co., 1845-60. Annual. Continued by:

The Indian Army and Civil Service list. Wm.H.Allen & Co., 1861-76. Continued by:

The India list, civil and military. Wm.H.Allen & Co., 1877-1900.

There are numerous other lists, arranged here in rough chronological order:

PHILLIPART, J. *The East India military calendar, containing the services of general and field officers of the Indian Army.* 3 vols. Kingsbury, Parbury and Allen, 1823-6. Military biographies of senior officers.

HARDY, CHARLES. *A register of ships employed in the service of the Honourable The East India Co., from the year 1706-1810 ...* 2 vols., revised Horatio Charles Hardy. Black, Parry and Kingsbury, 1811. Includes full lists of officers.

PRINSEP, CHARLES C. *Record of services of the Honourable East India Company's civil servants in the Madras Presidency from 1741 to 1858 ...* Trübner & Co., 1885.

SPRING, F.W.M. *The Bombay Artillery: list of officers who have served in the Bombay Artillery from its formation in 1749 to amalgamation with the Royal Artillery ...* William Clowes and Sons, 1902.

HODSON, V.C.P. *List of the officers of the Bengal army, 1758-1834.* 4 vols. Constable & Co., 1927-48. Includes biographical and genealogical notes.

DODWELL, EDWARD, & MILES, JAMES SAMUEL. *Alphabetical list of the officers of the Indian Army, with the dates of their respective promotion, retirement, resignation, or death, whether in India or Europe, from the year 1760 to the year 1834 inclusive, corrected to September 30, 1837.* Longman, Orme, Brown & Co., 1838.

DODWELL, EDWARD, & MILES, J.S. *Alphabetical list of the medical officers of the Indian Army, with the dates of their respective appointments, promotion, retirement, resignation or death, whether in Europe or India, from the year 1764 to the year 1838.* Longman, Orme, Brown and Co., 1839.

A list of the names of the members of the United Company of Merchants of England trading to the East Indies, who appear qualified to vote at their general courts. [East India Company?] 1773-1852. Many issues; title varies.

A list of the company's civil servants at their settlements in the East Indies, the island of Saint Helena, and China. [ ], 1782-99. 3 issues.

List of the East India Company's civil establishment on the coast of Coromandel, 1785. [ ], 1785.

A complete list of all the Honble. Company's servants in India, first of January, 1791. [ ], 1791.

THACKERAY, EDWARD T. *Biographical notices of officers of the Royal (Bengal) Engineers.* Smith, Elder & Co., 1900. Covers 1756-1890.

DODWELL, EDWARD, & MILES, JAMES SAMUEL. *Alphabetical list of the Honble. East India Company's Bengal civil servants, from the year 1780 to the year 1838, to which is attached a list of the Governor-Generals of India from the year 1773 to the year 1838. Also, a list of the East India directors, from the year 1775 to the year 1838.* Woking: [ ], 1838.

The Bengal calender for the year 1788, including a list of the Hon. and United East India Company's civil and military servants on the Bengal establishment, &c., including also those at Madras, Bombay, Fort Marlborough, China, and St. Helena. John Stockdale, 1787-8. 2 issues.

The Bengal calendar & register ... containing complete and accurate lists of the Honorable East India Company's servants on the Bengal establishment ... Calcutta: James White, 1790.

PRINSEP, H.T. *A general register of the honourable East India Company's civil servants of the Bengal establishment from 1790 to 1842, comprising the dates of their respective appointments, furloughs, retirements, deaths, etc., etc., alphabetically arranged...* Calcutta: Ramchundur Doss, 1844.

DODWELL, E., & MILES, J.S. *Alphabetical list of the Honourable East India Company's Bombay civil servants, from the year 1798 to the year 1839, distinguishing, with dates, the several high and important offices held by them during their official career, also the dates of their retirement, resignation or death, to which is attached a list of the governers of Bombay from the year 1773 to the year 1839 ...; also, a list of the East*

India directors from the year 1779 to the year 1839 ... Longman, Orme, Brown and Co., 1839.

CRAWFORD, D.G. *Roll of the Indian Medical Service, 1815-1930.* W.Thacker & Co., 1930.

DE RHÉ-PHILIPE, G.W. *Narrative of the first Burmese war, 1824-26 ...* Calcutta: Superintendant of Government Printing, 1905. Includes roll of officers killed, wounded or captured.

The army of the Sutlej, 1845-46 casualty roll. London Stamp Exchange, [1985?]

The Bombay Army list: also, Hyderabad Contingent list, the Indian Navy list, and the Bombay civil list, including the ecclesiastical establishment. Bombay: Bombay Education Society's Press, 1854-75. Title varies, published quarterly.

TAVENDER, I.T. *Casualty roll for the Indian Mutiny, 1857-59.* Polstead: J.B.Hayward & Son, 1983.

Medals

For medals, see:

GOULD, R.W., & DOUGLAS-MORRIS, K.J. *The Army of India medal roll 1799-1826.* J.B.Hayward & Son, 1974. Includes bibliography.

Honours and Awards, Indian Army: August 1914-August 1921. J.B.Hayward & Son, [199-?] Originally published as *Roll of Honour, Indian army 1914-1921.* 1931.

The Victoria Crosses and George Crosses of the Honourable East India Company and Indian Army, 1856-1945. National Army Museum, 1962. Lists recipients.

Monumental Inscriptions

Many monumental inscriptions relating to company employees are recorded in:

DE RHE-PHILIPE, GEORGE WILLIAM, & IRVING, MILES. *Soldiers of the Raj.* London Stamp Exchange, 1989. Reprints *A list of Christian tombs or monuments in the Punjab, North-West Frontier Province, Kashmir and Afghanistan, possessing historical or archeaological interest.* 2 vols. Indian monumental series 2. Lahore: Punjab Government Press, 1910. Includes as part II, 'Biographical notices of military officers and others whose names appear in the inscriptions in part II.

Electrical Tradesmen

ELECTRICAL REVIEW. *Electrical who's who.* Electrical Review Publications, 1950. There are more recent editions.

The Electricians directory, with diary for 18--. 2 vols. James Gray, 1883-4. Continued by: *The Electrician electrical trades directory and handbook for 18--.* The Electrician, 1890-1926.

Engineers

BELL, S. PETER. *A biographical index of British engineers in the 19th century.* New York: Garland, 1975. Indexes obituaries of some 3,500 engineers from pre-1901 journals.

Consulting engineer yearbook ... 4 vols. Princes Press, 1947-50.

DAY, M.E. *The engineer's who's who 1939: a register of engineering appointments and attainments.* 2nd ed. Dorking: The Engineers Who's Who, [1939].

JUNIOR INSTITUTION OF ENGINEERS. *List of members.* The Institution, 1934 & 1937. Lists for other years may also be available.

LOW, DAVID ALLAN. *The Whitworth book.* Longmans, Green and Co., 1926. Biographical dictionary of beneficiaries of the Whitworth Foundation (Engineers.)

Marchant & Co's metropolitan and provincial engineers, iron & metal trades directory for 1857, with which is incorporated the builders and building trades directory. Marchant Singer & Co., 1857.

PIKE, W.T. ed. *British engineers and allied professions in the twentieth century: contemporary biographies.* Pike's new century series **24.** Brighton: W.T.Pike & Co., 1908.

SEARS, JOHN ED. *Who's who in Engineering.* Compendium Publishing, 1920-21.

SHARP, ROBERT. *Obituaries of British engineers, 1901-1920: an alphabetical index.* Science Museum, 1993.

Who's who of British Engineers. Madaren & Sons, 1966. Many later editions.

See also Civil Engineers, Councillors, and Railway Engineers.

Engravers

ENGEN, RODNEY K. *Dictionary of Victorian engravers, print publishers and their work.* Cambridge: Chadwycke-Healey, 1979. Brief biographical notes, with detailed lists of works.

HUNNISETT, BASIL. *An illustrated dictionary of British steel engravers.* Aldershot: Scolar, 1989.

HUNNISETT, BASIL. *A dictionary of British steel engravers.* Leigh on Sea: F. Lewis, 1980.

SALAMAN, MALCOLM C. *The old engravers of England in their relation to contemporary life and art.* Cassell & Co., 1906. Includes much personal information on engravers, 1540-1800.

SYMONDS, HENRY. 'English mint engravers of the Tudor and Stuart periods, 1485 to 1688', *Numismatic chronicle* 4th series **13,** 1913, 349-77.

See also Artists and Coiners

Entertainers

See Actors

Entomologists

GILBERT, PAMELA. *A compendium of the biographical literature on deceased entomologists.* British Museum (Natural History), 1977.

Estate Agents

See Auctioneers

Etchers

GRANT, MAURICE HAROLD. *A dictionary of British etchers.* Rockliff, 1952. Brief biographical notes.

Exchequer Officials

SQUIBB, LAWRENCE. 'A book of all the several officers of the Court of the Exchequer, together with the names of the present officers, in whose gift, and how admitted ... January, 1641,' ed. William Hamilton Bryson. *Camden miscellany* **26.** Camden 4th series **14,** 1975, 77-136.

SAINTY, J.C. *Officers of the Exchequer.* Special series, **18.** List & Index Society, 1983- . List, with brief biographical notes, 12-19th c.

Explorers

SAVOURS, ANN. 'The manuscript collection of the Scott Polar Research Institute, Cambridge', *Archives* 4(22), 1959, 102-8. General description of collection, including list of journals and notebooks.

See also Merchants

Fanciers

BROWN, EDWARD. *The Fanciers directory, containing the names and addresses of all judges and exhibitors of dogs, poultry, cage birds, rabbits and cats in the United Kingdom, from April 1879 to March 1880.* Cassell, Petter, Galpin & Co., 1880.

Farmers

COLLINS, E.J.T. 'Historical farm records,' *Archives* 7(35), 1966, 143-9. General discussion.

Historical farm records: a summary guide to manuscripts and other material in the University Library collected by the Institute of Agricultural History and the Museum of English Rural Life. Reading: University of Reading Library, 1973. Lists a wide range of sources topographically, including some, e.g., accounts, diaries, etc., of potential genealogical interest.

Farriers

National registration of farriers: list of shoeing smiths registered by the Worshipful Company of Farriers. The Company, 1902.

Feminists

BANKS, OLIVE. *The biographical dictionary of British feminists.* 2 vols. Brighton: Wheatsheaf, 1985-90. vol.1: 1800-1930. vol.2. A supplement, 1900-1945.

Firearms makers

See Gunmakers

Firemen

KLOPPER, HARRY. *Who's who in the fire services, and fire brigades directory.* 2nd ed. Fire, 1958/9.

Fishermen

BAKER, ROBERT. 'Was your ancestor a fisherman?' *Family tree magazine* 5(8), 1989, 8-9. Discusses useful records at the Public Record Office.

Fishmongers

The British fisheries directory, 1883-4. Sampson, Low, Marston, Searle & Rivington, 1883. Topographical directory of tradesmen such as boat builders, fishmongers, sailmakers, fishing tackle manufacturers, ropemakers, shell-fish merchants, fish curers, salt merchants, *etc.*

PHILIPS, G. *The fish, poultry, game and rabbit senders directory, containing names and addresses of country senders of fish, salmon, shell fish, shrimps, prawns, lobsters, crabs, poultry, game and rabbit senders, and importers of Russian and Norwegian game.* Exeter: G.Phillips, 1890.

Footballers

EMMS, STEVE & MCPHERSON, DAVE. *Who's who of the Football League 1919-1939.* Basildon: Association of Football Statisticians, 1993- . 7 parts to date.

GLANVILLE, BRIAN. *Empire News footballers who's who.* 2nd ed. Manchester: Kemsley Newspapers, [1954?] 2,190 brief biographies.

Who's who of the Football League, 1888- 1915. Basildon: Association of Football Statisticians, 1994- . 10 parts to date.

Foundrymen

INSTITUTE OF BRITISH FOUNDRYMEN. *List of members ...* The Institute, 1933-46. 9 vols.

Framework Knitters

GODDARD, J.R. 'Was your ancestor an F.W.K.?' *Family tree magazine* 6(4), 1990, 4-5, & 6(5), 1990, 4-5. Framework knitters.

Freemasons

KNOOP, DOUGLAS, & JONES, G.P. *A handlist of Masonic documents.* Manchester University Press, 1942. Lists numerous sources for freemasons.

Who's who in freemasonry (1913-14). Lever Press, c.1913.

Freemen

CLARK, DAVID. 'Freemen of England and Wales', *Family tree magazine* 9(3), 1993, 41-2.

WARD, HARRY. *Freemen in England.* Epsom: Harry Ward, 1975. Brief notes on the history of freemen in 58 boroughs.

WOODWARD, D.M. 'Sources for modern history, 1: freemens' rolls', *Local historian* 9, 1970-71, 89-95. General discussion of sources.

Fruiterers

The 'Fruit Grower' directory and handbook.
Benn Bros., 1921-5. Annual. Includes extensive
lists of fruiterers, *etc.*

Furniture makers

BEARD, GEOFFREY, & GILBERT, CHRISTOPHER,
eds. *Dictionary of English furniture makers,
1660-1840.* Leeds: Furniture History Society,
with W. S. Maney & Son, 1986. Indexed in:
EVANS, ANGELA. *Index to the dictionary of
English furniture makers.* Furniture History
Society, 1990- .
*The furnishing trade encyclopedia, who's who,
diary and buyers guide.* Furnishing World,
1936-65. Title varies.
*The Post Office directory of the cabinet,
furniture and upholstery trades and the
trades connected therewith.* Kelly & Co.,
1877-1936. 12 editions. Title varies; from 1886
became *Kelly's directory of ...*
See also Silversmiths.

Gardeners

See Horticulturalists

Gas Workers

LOVERSEED, DAVID. *Gas worker ancestors: how
to find out more about them: a guide to
genealogical sources for the British Gas
industry.* Stockport: D.C.S., 1994.
Gaslight. Manchester: North West Gas
Historical Society, 1990. Newsletter.

Geologists

GEOLOGICAL SOCIETY OF LONDON. *List of
officers and members.* The Society, 1835- .
Title varies.
SCIENCE MUSEUM LIBRARY. *A bibliography of
British geologists who died between 1850
and 1900.* Bibliographical series, **801.** The
Library, 1972. Includes obituaries.

Gipsies

Register of traveller research. South Chailey:
Romany & Traveller Family History Society,
1995. Includes information on various resources, as well as a listing of members' research interests.

Goldsmiths

CHAFFERS, WILLIAM. *Gilda aurifabrorum: a
history of English goldsmiths and
plateworkers and their marks stamped on
plate copied in facsimile from celebrated
examples, and the earliest examples
preserved at Goldsmith Hall, London, with
their names, addresses, and dates of entry ...*
W.H.Allen & Co., 1883.
CULME, JOHN. *Directory of gold and
silversmiths, jewellers and allied traders 1838-
1914, from the London Assay Office
registers.* 2 vols. Woodbridge: Antique
Collectors Club, 1987.
EVANS, JOAN. 'Huguenot goldsmiths in England
and Ireland', *Proceedings of the Huguenot
Society of London* **14,** 1930-33, 496-554.
Includes list.
HOPE, ROBERT CHARLES. *English goldsmiths
who have been or still are members of the
goldsmiths' companies in the cities or towns
where plate is or was assayed.* Bemrose and
Sons, [18--.]
HOPE, ROBERT CHARLES. 'English goldsmiths',
Reliquary N.S., **2,** 1888, 218-23; **3,** 1889, 31-40,
74-88, 159-67, & 241-5; **4,** 1890, 24-34. In
London, York, Newcastle on Tyne, and
Chester.
PRIOR, MATTHEW. 'The goldsmiths' halls in the
provinces in 1773', *Reliquary* N.S., **7,** 1893,
21-7. Includes list of Chester and Newcastle
on Tyne goldsmiths, with Exeter assay office
accounts giving names.
JACKSON, CHARLES JAMES, SIR. *English
Goldsmiths and thier marks: a history of the
goldsmiths and plate workers of England,
Scotland, and Ireland ...* 2nd ed. B.T.Batsford,
1921. Includes lists; extensive.
LEVER, CHRISTOPHER. *Goldsmiths and
silversmiths of England.* Hutchinson, 1975.
Most chapters deal with prominent
goldsmiths; includes pedigreee of De
Lamerie, 17th-19th century.
PICKFORD, IAN, ed. *Jackson's silver & gold
marks of England, Scotland and Ireland.* 3rd
ed. Woodbridge: Antique Collectors Club,
1989. Includes extensive lists of gold and
silver smiths.
SITWELL, H. D. W. 'The Jewel House and the
royal goldsmiths', *Archaeological journal*
117, 1960, 131-55. Includes lists, 16-19th c.
See also Silversmiths

Golfers

ALLISS, PETER. *The who's who of golf.* Orbis Publishing, 1983.

Golfers handbook. [ ]: Munro-Barr, 1898- . Includes who's who.

Who's who in golf, and directory of golf clubs and members. Watts Burton & Co., 1908-13. Title and publisher vary.

Grocers

See Wine and Spirit Trades

Gunmakers

BAILEY, DE WITT, & NIE, DOUGLAS A. *English gunmakers: the Birmingham and provincial gun trade in the 18th and 19th centuries.* Arms & Armour Press, 1978. Includes list of gunmakers, giving places and dates.

CAREY, ARTHUR MERWYN. *English, Irish and Scottish firearms makers: when, where and what they made, from the middle of the sixteenth century to the end of the nineteenth century.* 2nd ed. Arms & Armour Press, 1967. List with brief biographical notes.

KENNARD, A.N. *Gunfounding and gunfounders: a directory of cannon founders from earliest times to 1850.* Arms & Armour Press, 1986.

NEAL, W.KEITH, & BACK, D.H.L. *British gunmakers: their trade cards, cases and equipment, 1760-1860.* Warminster: Compton Press, 1980. Includes some biographical information.

Gunpowder Manufacturers

WEST, JENNY. *Gunpowder, government and war in the mid-eighteenth century.* Studies in history **63**. Boydell Press for the Royal Historical Society, 1991. Gives descents of various gunpowder mills.

Hangmen

BLAND, JAMES. *The common hangman: English and Scottish hangmen before the abolition of public execution.* Hornchurch: Ian Henry Publications, 1984. Popular account.

Hatters

The hatters' gazette, diary and trade directory. Trade Journals, 1890-1951. Title and publisher vary.

Heretics

STUBBS, W. 'A calender of authenticated trials for heresy in England prior to the year 1533, stating in tabular form the name of the accused, the date of the trial ...', in *Report of the commissioners appointed to enquire into the conditions and working of the ecclesiastical courts ...* Vol. 1. House of Commons sessional papers 1883, **XXIV**, 52-69.

Hop Growers

See Wine and Spirit Trades

Horsemen

Tote investors' who's who in racing. Tote Investors, 1939. Extensive.

Horticulturalists

HADFIELD, MILES, HARLING, ROBERT, & HIGHTON, LEONIE. *British gardeners: a biographical dictionary.* A. Zwemmer, 1980. Includes biographies of 500 gardeners.

HARVEY, JOHN. *Early nurserymen.* Phillimore, 1974. Includes various wills and inventories, with a list of London nurserymen and seedsmen.

HARVEY, JOHN. *Early horticultural catalogues: a checklist of trade catalogues, issued by firms of nurserymen and seedsmen in Great Britain and Ireland down to the year 1850.* Bath: University of Bath Library, 1973. Includes addresses and dates of many individual nurserymen, and notes changes of firms' names.

WILLSON, E.J. 'Commercial gardening records, I: the records of nurserymen', *Archives* 12(55), 1976, 121-6. General discussion.

The horticultural directory. Journal of Horticulture, 1867-1934. Mainly annual; publisher varies. Alphabetical list, by London and counties, of seedsmen, gardeners and nurserymen.

See also Botanists

Hoteliers

BIRD-DAVIS, C.H. *Who's who in the hotel world and hotel keepers vade mecum.* World's Hotel Blue Book, 1912.

See also Actors, and Wine and Spirit Trades

Household Officials

DE BEER, E.S. 'A list of the Department of the Lord Chamberlain of the Household, Autumn 1663', *Bulletin of the Institute of Historical Research* **19,** 1941, 13-24. Lists members of the royal household.

Huntsmen

Bailey's hunting directory. Vinton & Co., 1897- . Almost annual; title varies. Lists masters, secretaries and hunt servants.

British hunts and huntsmen: containing a short history of each fox and stag hunt in the British Isles, together with biographical records of masters past and present ... 4 vols. Biographical Press, 1908-11.

Hydrographers

DAY, ARCHIBALD, SIR. *The Admiralty Hydrographic Service, 1795-1919.* H.M.S.O., 1967. Includes chronological list of Hydrographical Dept. senior officers.

DAWSON, LLEWELLYN STYLES. *Memoirs of hydrography, including brief biographies of the principal officers who have served in H.M. Naval Survey Service between the years 1750 and 1885.* 2 vols. Eastbourne: H.W. Keay, 1883-5. 2,000 biographies.

Hymn Writers

HAYDEN, ANDREW J.,& NEWTON, ROBERT F. *British hymn-writers and composers: a checklist, giving their dates and places of birth and death.* Croydon: Hymn Society of Great Britain and Ireland, 1977.

JULIAN, JOHN. *A dictionary of hymnology ... with biographical and critical notices ...* John Murray, 1892. Many brief biographies.

THOMSON, RONALD W. *Who's who of hymn writers.* Epworth Press, 1967.

Industrialists

MURPHY, WILLIAM S. *Captains of industry.* Glasgow: The author, 1903. Biographical portraits of industrialists.

SMILES, SAMUEL. *Industrial biography: iron workers and tool makers.* John Murray, 1863. Reprinted Newton Abbot: David & Charles, 1967. Biographical accounts of leading industrialists.

See also Scientists.

Inland Revenue Officers

Inland Revenue establishment: Chief Inspector's Branch. Clerical establishment. H.M.S.O., 1921.

Inland Revenue Department. Chief Inspector's Branch. Tax inspectorate, 1st April, 1929. Eyre & Spottiswoode, 1929. Lists tax inspectors.

Innkeepers

See Publicans

Instrument Makers

See Mathematicians

Insurance Policy Holders

From the late eighteenth century onwards, insurance records contain much information of genealogical value. A comprehensive introduction is provided by:

COCKERELL, H.A.L., & GREEN, EDWIN. *The British Insurance business, 1547-1970: an introduction and guide to historical records in the United Kingdom.* Heinemann, 1976. This also includes information on staff records.

The uses of insurance records are discussed in:

JACKSON, T.V. 'The Sun Fire Office and the local historian', *Local historian* **17**(3), 1986, 141-9.

DICKENSON, M.J. 'Insurance policy registers', *Bulletin of local history: East Midlands Region* **6** 1971, 42-50. Brief.

Lists of names are to be found in:

EDWARDS, L.W. LAWSON. 'Sun Fire Insurance Office claims 1770-1788', *Genealogists' magazine* **18,** 1975-6, 193-201. Includes list of claimants.

JENKINS, D.T. *Index of the fire insurance policies of the Sun Fire Office and the Royal Exchange Assurance, 1775-1787.* Guildhall Library, [1986].

Insurers

CAVERLEY, R.B., & BANKES, R.B. *Leading insurance men of the British Empire.* Index Pub. Co., 1892.

DICKSON, P.G.M. *The Sun Insurance Office, 1710-1960: the history of two and a half centuries of British insurance.* O.U.P., 1960. Includes brief lists of officers, also useful, if brief, bibliography.

*Insurance who's who: a biographical dictionary
of the principal officials of British insurance
companies ...* Insurance News, 1924-34?

*A list of the subscribers to Lloyds, also a list
of the agents and a copy of their
appointment and instructions ...* 9 issues. W.
Hughes, 1833-49. Publisher varies.

*The Post magazine almanack and court and
Parliamentary register.* W.S.D.Pateman, 1842-
93. Annual; title varies. Primarily an
insurance directory, listing many names of
insurers, *etc.*

Inventors

WOODCROFT, BENNET. *Brief biographies of
inventors of machines for the manufacture of
textile fabrics.* Longman, Green, Longmans,
Roberts & Green, 1863.

See also Patentees.

Iron Workers

TYLER, PETER M. 'Old occupations: iron
workers', *Family tree magazine* **9**(8-10), 1993,
passim.

Ironmongers

Rylands directory of ironmongers.
Birmingham: Iron Trades Circular (Rylands),
1900-4. 2 issues.

Jacobite Rebels

See Landowners.

Jesuits

See Monks and Religious Orders

Jockeys

MARCH, RUSSELL. *The jockeys of Vanity Fair.*
Tunbridge Wells: March Publications, 1985.
Includes biographies of jockeys.

MORTIMER, ROGER, ONSLOW, RICHARD, &
WILLETT, PETER. *Biographical encyclopaedia
of British flat racing.* Macdonald and Jane's,
1978. Includes horses as well as the jockeys!

Journalists

INSTITUTE OF JOURNALISTS. *Officers of the
Institute. The Council. District and local
organisation. List of members. Professional
register of members.* 1913-23. 7 vols.
Continued as *Grey book.* 1928- . Post-war
issues do not include the extensive 'roll of
members' printed in earlier editions.

NATIONAL UNION OF JOURNALISTS. *A directory
of free-lance news and specialist
correspondents.* [National Union of
Journalists], 1939.

TRACEY, HERBERT, ed. *The British press: a
survey, a newspaper directory, and a who's
who in journalism.* Europa Publications,
1929.

Who's who in press, publicity, printing.
Cosmopolitan Press, 1939.

Judges

See Lawyers.

Justices of the Peace

GLEASON, J.H. *The justices of the peace in
England, 1558 to 1640.* Oxford: Clarendon
Press, 1969. Includes various lists of J.P.'s.

PUTNAM, B.H. 'Justices of the Peace for 1558-
1688', *Bulletin of the Institute of Historical
Research* **4**, 1926-7. 144-56. Identifies lists of
J.P.'s in the public records.

VERDUYN, A. 'The selection and appointment of
Justices of the Peace in 1338', *Historical
research* **68**(165), 1995, 1-25. Includes lists of
men nominated and appointed.

See also Councillors

King's Counsel

See Lawyers

King's Messengers

WHEELER-HOLOHAN, A.V. *The history of the
King's Messengers.* Grayson & Grayson, 1935.
Includes nominal roll of the King's
Messengers, 1641 to 1932.

Knights

SHAW, W.A. *The knights of England.* 2 vols.
Shervatt & Hughes, 1906. Lists all creations
to 1904.

MOOR, C., ed. *Knights of Edward I.* 5 vols.
Publications of the Harleian Society **80-84.**
1929-32. Biographical dictionary.

FELLOWES, EDMUND HORACE. *The Knights of
the Garter 1348-1939, with a complete list of
the stall-plates in St George's Chapel.*
S.P.C.K., for the Dean and Canon of St
George's Chapel in Windsor Castle, [1939].

FELLOWES, EDMUND H. *The military Knights
of Windsor, 1352-1944.* Windsor: Oxley and
Sons for the Dean and Canon of St George's
Chapel, 1944. Brief biographies of numerous
'Knights'.

Knights *continued*

WINTHROP, WILLIAM. 'The English, Irish and Scotch Knights of the order of St John of Jerusalem', *Notes and queries* **200**, 1853, 189-92. 16th c. list.

For works on the Peerage, Baronetage *etc.,* see Raymond's *English Genealogy: a bibliography,* section 7.

Labour Movement Workers

BELLAMY, JOYCE M., & SAVILLE, JOHN. *Dictionary of labour biography.* 8 vols. Macmillan, 1972-86. Each volume is arranged alphabetically; v.8 contains a consolidated list of names.

BIRD, STEPHEN. 'Archives of the working class movement: a national collection in Manchester', *Manchester region history review* 5(2), 1991/2, 31-4.

FOWLER, SIMON. *Sources for labour history.* Labour Heritage, 1991. Includes chapter on 'records for family historians and biographers.'

KNIGHT, GERALDINE. 'The Working Class Movement Library', *Manchester region history review* 3(1), 1989, 82-5. The library includes much material on trade unionists, *etc.*

The labour who's who 1924: a biographical directory to the national and local leaders in the Labour and Co-operative movement. Labour Publishing Co., 1924. 2nd ed., 1927.

See also Politicians

Lacemakers

CAMERON, ALAN. 'The records of the Lacemakers Company', *Bulletin of local history: East Midland region* **12**, 1977, 12-16. Mainly concerned with the East Midlands. Membership registers exist 1900-1971.

Land Agents

See Auctioneers and Surveyors

Landowners

Printed sources for tracing landowners are numerous, and a volume should be written on tracing landowners and their family trees. Local sources are listed in the county volumes of *British genealogical bibliographies.* Here, it is only possible to list a handful of titles of general use. They are arranged in chronological order. The most important early source is, of course, Domesday Book. This has been much studied, and the resultant literature is listed in:

BATES, DAVID. *A bibliography of Domesday Book.* Woodbridge: Boydell Press for the Royal Historical Society, 1981.

During the medieval period, an *inquisition post mortem* was taken on the death of a tenant in chief. These documents list his lands, and give his heir(s). They are being published in:

Calendar of inquisition post mortem and other documents preserved in the Public Record Office. H.M.S.O., 1898- . In progress. Currently, 19 volumes cover the years 1235-1405, and 3 volumes the years 1485-1509.

Identifying the tenants of medieval landlords is the subject of:

PARK, B. *My ancestors were manorial tenants: how can I find out more about them?* Society of Genealogists, 1990.

During the Civil War and Interregnum, royalist 'delinquents' had to pay substantial fines from their estates to 'compound' for their delinquency. Full details of these fines, and of the proceedings of the Parliamentary committee which administered them, are given (not always accurately) in:

GREEN, MARY ANNE EVERETT, ed. *Calendar of the proceedings of the Committee for Compounding, &c., 1643-1660 ...* 5 vols. H.M.S.O., 1889-92. Reprinted Nendeln, Liechtenstein: Kraus Reprint, 1967.

Valuable information on landowners who supported the Stuart cause in 1715 is provided by:

ESTCOURT, EDGAR E., & PAYNE, JOHN ORLEBAR, eds. *The English Catholic nonjurors of 1715, being a summary of the register of their estates, with genealogical and many other notes, and an appendix of unpublished documents in the Public Record Office.* Thomas Baker, 1900.

For estates forfeited in the '45 Jacobite rebellion, see:

The records of the Forfeited Estates Commission. Public Record Office handbooks, 12. H.M.S.O., 1968.

The major sources of information on landowners in the 17-19th c. are the surveys conducted for enclosure purposes, and, later, for tithe redemption. See:

BREWER, J.G. *Enclosures and the open fields: a bibliography.* Reading: British Agricultural History Society, 1972. Lists many works on enclosure, some of which include transcripts of awards.

TATE, W.E. *A Domesday of English enclosure acts and awards.* Reading: University of Reading Library, 1978. Lists awards.

KAIN, R.J.P. *An atlas and index of tithe files of mid-nineteenth century England and Wales.* Cambridge: C.U.P., 1980.

Inland Revenue tithe maps and apportionments (I.R. 29, I.R. 30). 2 vols. List & Index Society, **68 & 83.** 1971-2. List of documents in the Public Record Office.

Land tax records are also of great value; see:

GIBSON, J.S.W., MEDLYCOTT, M., & MILLS, D. *Land and window tax assessments.* Birmingham: F.F.H.S., 1993.

The most comprehensive national survey of landownership was undertaken in the early 1870's; the consequent Parliamentary return claims to list everyone who owned more than 1 acre:

Owners of land, 1872-73 (England and Wales). 2 vols. House of Commons Parliamentary papers 1874, **72,** pts.1 & 2. (C1097). H.M.S.O., 1874.

See also:

BATEMAN, JOHN. *The great landowners of Great Britain and Ireland: a list of all owners of three thousand acres and upwards, worth £3,000 a year, in England, Scotland, Wales and Ireland, their acreage, income from land, college, club, and services, culled from the Modern Domesday Book.* 4th ed. Harrison, 1883. Reprinted Leicester: Leicester U.P., 1971.

The records of a more recent survey are discussed in:

SHORT, BRIAN, & REED, MICK. 'An Edwardian land survey: the Finance (1909-10) Act 1910 records', *Journal of the Society of Archivists* 8(2), 1986, 95-103.

Land Surveyors
See Surveyors

Laundry Trades
The laundry trade directory and launderers handbook with diary. Laundry Record Office, 1908.

Kelly's directory of the laundry and allied trades ... throughout England Scotland and Wales. Kelly's Directories, 1934-8. 2 issues.

Lawyers
There is a book waiting to be written on the genealogical and biographical study of lawyers - that is barristers, solicitors, judges, advocates, etc. Much information is available in print, and the works listed here are merely the tip of the iceberg. More titles may be identified in:

BLAND, D.S. *A bibliography of the Inns of Court and Chancery.* Supplementary series **3.** Selden Society, 1965.

See also:

WOOLLAM, E.R. 'Sources of legal biography: a selective description', *North West Kent family history* 1(4), 1979, 92-6. Brief but useful bibliographical essay.

Lists of lawyers were — and still are — regularly published. See:

Lists of attornies and solicitors admitted in pursuance of the late act for the better regulation of attornies and solicitors ... 1729. Richard Williamson, 1729. Continued by the extensive *Additional lists of attornies and solicitors ...* 1730.

Lists of the officers and their deputies belonging to the several courts in Westminster Hall and elsewhere, with the lists, accounts and tables of fees claimed by them which were presented to the House of Commons ... 1730. Richard Williamson, 1730.

BROWNE, JOHN. *Browne's general law list for the year 17--, with the names and residences of all the judges and sergeants, King's counsel & barristers ... [etc].* John Browne and J. Butterworth, 1777-97.

New law list. 1798-1802. Continued by *Clarke's new law list: being a list of the judges and officers of the different courts of justice: counsel, special pleaders, conveyancers ... attornies, notaries, &c., in England and Wales.* W. Clarke & Sons, 1803-40, and by *The Law List ...* W. Clarke & Sons, et al., 1841- . Lists barristers, solicitors, etc., with addresses and qualifications.

The solicitor's diary, almanack and legal directory. Waterloo (London), 1844-[1984?]

The lawyer's companion and diary, and London and provincial directory for 18--. Stevens & Son, 1847-1975. Annual. Title and publisher varies. Early issues include 'a list of the English bar', and of various legal officers, etc.

The Incorporated Law Society calendar. The Society, 1881-95. Annual. Includes extensive lists of lawyers.

INCORPORATED LAW SOCIETY. *Law Society's registry.* 1888-1902. Continued as *The Law Society gazette.* 1903- . The *Registry* was published as a supplement and includes a 'list of gentlemen applying to be admitted as solicitors', etc.

Record of service of solicitors and articled clerks with his majesty's forces 1914-1919. Spottiswoode, Ballantyne & Co., 1920. Alphabetical list, extensive.

Butterworth's Empire law list. Butterworth & Co., 1921-58. Issued with the annual supplement to *Halsbury's laws of England.* Lists firms, giving names of partners.

List of barristers returned to practice from war service. General Council of the Bar, 1947.

Various biographical dictionaries, etc., are available:

BAKER, J.H. *The order of serjeants at law: a chronicle of creations, with related text and a historical introduction.* Selden Society supplementary series, 5. 1984. Includes list, 1267-1875.

BAKER, J.H. 'The bookplates of serjeants at law', *The bookplate journal* 3(2), 1985, 65-82. List with biographical notes.

CAMPBELL, JOHN. *The lives of the chief justices of England from the Norman conquest till the death of Lord Tenterden,* ed. James Cockcroft. New ed. 5 vols. Northport, New York: E.Thompson Co., 1894-9.

COOTE, CHARLES. *Sketches of the lives and characters of eminent English civilians, with an historical introduction relative to the College of Advocates and an enumeration of the whole series of academic graduates admitted into that Society from the beginning of the reign of Henry VIII to the close of the year 1803.* G. Kearsley, 1804.

FOSS, EDWARD. *The judges of England, with sketches of their lives, and miscellaneous notices connected with the courts at Westminster from the time of the Conquest.* 9 vols. Longman, Brown, Green & Longmans,

1848-64. A one-volume abridgement of this work is provided by: *Biographia juridica: a biographical dictionary of the judges of England, from the Conquest to the present time, 1066-1870.* John Murray, 1870.

FOSTER, JOSEPH. *Men-at-the-bar: a biographical handlist of the members of the various Inns of Court, including Her Majesty's judges, etc.* Collectanea genealogica 12. Reeves & Turner, 1885.

HARDY, THOMAS D. *A catalogue of lords chancellors, keepers of the Great Seal, masters of the rolls, and principal officers of the Court of Chancery.* H. Butterworth, 1843.

HEUSTON, R.F.V. *Lives of the Lord Chancellors, 1885-1939.* Oxford: Clarendon Press, 1964.

HEUSTON, R.F.V. *Lives of the Lord Chancellors 1940-1970.* Oxford: Clarendon Press, 1987.

PREST, WILFRED R. *The rise of the barristers: a social history of the English bar, 1590-1640.* Oxford: Clarendon Press, 1986. Includes extensive 'biographical notes on benchers'.

SAINTY, JOHN, SIR. *A list of English law officers, Kings Counsel, and holders of patents of precedence.* Supplementary series 7. Selden Society, 1987.

SIMPSON, A.W.B. *Biographical dictionary of the common law.* Butterworths, 1984.

WOOLRYCH, HUMPHRY WILLIAM. *Lives of eminent serjeants at law of the English bar.* 2 vols. Wm. H. Allen & Co., 1869. Brief biographies of 58 serjeants.

The records of the Inns of Court provide a great deal of information on lawyers — and also on those who needed a smattering of legal knowledge to run their estates, conduct manorial business, and take part in local government. The Inns were not just for intending lawyers, but catered for many who followed careers in other fields. Consequently, every genealogist should consult at least the registers of admissions to the Inns. For a list of manuscript and published sources, see:

BLAND, D.S. 'The records of the Inns of Court: a bibliographical aid', *Amateur historian* 5(3), 1962, 72-6.

American members are listed in:

JONES, E. ALFRED. *American members of the Inns of Court.* St. Catherine Press, 1924. Includes many brief biographies.

For interesting and scholarly studies of the inns, see:

LEMMINGS, DAVID. *Gentlemen and barristers: the Inns of Court and the English bar, 1680-1730.* Oxford: Clarendon Press, 1990. Includes useful bibliography.

PREST, WILFRED R. *The Inns of Court under Elizabeth I and the early Stuarts, 1590-1640.* Longman, 1972. Scholarly general study, includes a 'note on archival sources'.

Clements Inn
CARR, CECIL, SIR, ed. *Pension book of Clements Inn.* Selden Society, **78.** 1960. Includes list of members, with their sureties, 1658-1883.

Doctors' Commons
SQUIBB, G.D. *Doctors' Commons: a history of the College of Advocates and Doctors of Law.* Oxford: Clarendon Press, 1977. Includes a register of members, 15th c.-1852.

Grays Inn
FLETCHER, REGINALD J., ed. *The pension book of Gray's Inn (records of the Honourable Society) 1569-[1800]).* 2 vols. Chiswick Press, 1901-10. Includes many names, with a list of treasurers, 1531-1909, and list of occupants of Gray's Inn, 1668.

FOSTER, JOSEPH. *The register of admissions to Gray's Inn, 1521-1889, together with the register of marriages in Gray's Inn Chapel, 1695-1754.* Hansard Publishing Union, 1889.

BIRKENHEAD, VISCOUNT. *The war book of Gray's Inn, containing names of members who served, with biographical notices of those who fell ...* Butterworth & Co., 1921.

Inner Temple
INDERWICK, F.A., & ROBERTS, R.A., eds. *A calendar of the Inner Temple records.* 5 vols. Henry Sotheran & Co., et al., 1896-1937. Includes subsidy roll, 1523, for the Inns of Court, Chancery, and officers of the courts of law, together with a register of burials in the Inner Temple, 1628-60. Also includes many other names.

Lincoln's Inn
BAILDON, WILLIAM. *Records of the Honourable Society of Lincoln's Inn: admissions 1420-1893, and chapel registers.* 2 vols. Lincoln's Inn, 1896.

BAILDON, W.P., ed. *The records of the Society of Lincoln's Inn: the black books.* 4 vols. H.S. Cartwright for the Society, 1897-1902. Includes many names, with notes on heraldry, list of calls to the bar, and of painters & engravers, etc.

Middle Temple
HUTCHINSON, JOHN. *A catalogue of notable Middle Templars, with brief biographical notices.* Butterworth, 1902.

INGPEN, ARTHUR ROBERT. *The Middle Temple bench books, being a register of benchers of the Middle Temple from the earliest records to the present time, with historical introduction.* Chiswick Press, 1912. Includes lists of treasurers, masters, readers, etc., with brief biographical notes.

STURGESS, H.A.C. *Register of admissions to the Honourable Society of the Middle Temple, from the fifteenth century to the year 1944.* Butterworth, for the Society, 1949.

MARTIN, CHARLES TRICE, ed. *Middle Temple records.* 4 vols. Butterworth, 1904-5. Minutes of Parliament, 1501-1703. Includes many names.

WILLIAMSON, J. BRUCE. *The Middle Temple bench book: being a register of benchers of the Middle Temple from the earliest records to the present time, with historical introduction.* 2nd ed. Chancery Lane Press, 1937. Includes various lists of officers.

See also Notaries Public, and Parliamentarians

Lay Readers
HUNT, W. HENRY. *The lay reader's official directory, 1906, containing a complete list of all licensed, diocesan, parochial and stipendiary readers in communion with the Church of England ...* W.H.Lord & Co., 1906.

Lead Miners
PASSMORE, SUE CAMPBELL. 'Old occupations: leadminers', *Family tree magazine* **9**(1), 1992, 4-5; **9**(2), 1992, 43-5.

Leather Trades
Kelly's directory of the leather trades ... Kelly & Co., 1871-1940. 20 issues.

Leather Trades *continued*

Board of Trade Containers and Straps (Leather and Textile) Order, 1943: list of persons whose names were on 14th February 1943 entered on the register of manufacturers of leather or textile containers and straps under the above order. H.M.S.O., 1943.

See also Business Records

Librarians

COLLISON, ROBERT L. *Who's who in librarianship.* Cambridge: Bowes & Bowes, [1954].

LANDAU, THOMAS. *Who's who in librarianship.* 2nd ed. Abelard Schuman, 1972.

KEELING, DENNIS F., ed. *British library history: bibliography 1962-1968.* Library Association, 1972. Further volumes cover publications of 1969-72, 1973-6, 1977-80, 1981-84 & 1985-8. Lists many biographies and obituaries.

Library Association year book. Library Association, 1891- . Includes lists of members.

Lifeboat Benefactors

TALBOT, MARY. 'Royal National Lifeboat Institution legacy papers', *Hampshire family historian* 6(1), 1979, 21-2; 6(2), 1979, 46-8. Lists testators, *etc.,* 1920s.

Local Government Officers

See Clerks of the Counties and Councillors.

Lord Chancellors

See Lawyers

Lord Lieutenants

SAINTY, J.C. *List of lieutenants of counties of England and Wales, 1660-1974.* Special series 12. List & Index Society, 1979. List with brief notes on appointments, etc.

Magistrates

See Councillors and Justices of the Peace.

Manorial Tenants

PARK, PETER. *My ancestors were manorial tenants.* 2nd ed. Society of Genealogists, 1994.

For other works on manorial records, consult Raymond's *English genealogy: a bibliography,* section 16A.

Martyrs (Roman Catholic)

BURTON, EDWIN H., & POLLEN, J.H. *Lives of the English martyrs. Second series. The martyrs declared venerable. Volume I: 1583-1588.* Longmans, Green & Co., 1914. No more published.

CAMM, BEDE, ed. *Lives of the English martyrs declared blessed by Pope Leo XIII in 1886 and 1895.* 2 vols. Burns & Oates, 1904-5. v.1. Martyrs under Henry VIII. v.2. Martyrs under Queen Elizabeth.

The Catholic martyrs of England and Wales: a chronological list of English and Welsh Martyrs who gave their lives for Christ during the penal times (A.D. 1535-1680 ...) Catholic Truth Society, 1979.

LAW, THOMAS GRAVES. *A calendar of the English martyrs of the sixteenth and seventeenth centuries.* Burns and Oates, 1876.

Masons

BURGESS, FREDERICK. *English churchyard memorials.* Lutterworth Press, 1963. Includes 'index of monumental stone carvers'.

BURGESS, FREDERICK. 'Country masons: a field of biographical research', *Genealogists' magazine* 11, 1951-4, 274-80.

SALZMAN, L.F. *Building in England down to 1540: a documented history.* Corrected impression. Oxford: Clarenden Press, 1966. Includes transcripts of numerous contracts made with masons.

SHELBY, LON R. 'The education of medieval English master masons', *Mediaeval studies* 32, 1970, 1-26. Study of literacy based on potentially useful sources.

WILLIAMS, W.J. 'Wills of freemasons and masons', *Masonic record* 16(181-91), 1935-6. Lists wills of masons, 1288-1600.

See also Architects

Masters of the Rolls

See Lawyers.

Mathematicians

TAYLOR, E.G.R. *The mathematical practitioners of Tudor and Stuart England.* Cambridge: C.U.P., 1954. Includes notices of 582 mathematicians.

TAYLOR, E.G.R. *The mathematical practitioners of Hanoverian England, 1714-1840.* Cambridge: C.U.P., 1966. Notes on over 2,700 individuals, mainly makers of instruments. Indexed in: BOSTOCK, KATE, HURT, SUSAN, & HURT, MICHAEL. *An index to the mathematical practitioners of Hanoverian England, 1714-1840.* H. Wynter, 1980.

WALLIS, R.V., & WALLIS, P.J. *Index of British mathematicians vol III: 1701-1800.* Newcastle-upon-Tyne: Project for Historical Biobibliography, 1993. Replaces and extends part II. Part I not published.

Mayors and Aldermen

BARNES, F.A. *The mayors of England & Wales, 1902.* Brighton: W.T.Pike & Co., 1902. Biographies.

MACKENZIE, DONALD, ed. *Mayors and Aldermen of Great Britain, and provosts and bailies of Scotland.* Sir J. Causton, 1935. Lists almost 4,000 men in office in 1935, with biographies and lists of mayors, 1910-34.

See also Councillors

Medical men

The records of the medical profession are voluminous, as is the printed material, and only a small selection can be listed here. The essential guide is:

BOURNE, SUSAN, & CHICKEN, ANDREW H. *Records of the medical professions: a practical guide for the family historian.* [Northfleet: S.Bourne], 1994.

A brief general discussion is provided by:

NEWMAN, CHARLES. 'Medical records', *Archives* 4(21), 1959, 1-8.

For surgeons, see also:

CARTER, MARY. 'Old occupations: surgeons', *Family tree magazine* 9(11), 1993, 15-16.

For a useful bibliography, see:

THORNTON, JOHN L. *A select bibliography of medical biography.* 2nd ed. Library Association, 1970. Includes a much more extensive list of collective biographies than that given below, and identifies many individual biographies.

A number of general biographical dictionaries and lists are available, and are listed here in chronological order:

KEALEY, EDWARD J. *Medieval medicus: physicians and health care in England, 1100-1154.* Baltimore: Johns Hopkins U.P., 1981. Includes biographical sketches of 90 physicians.

TALBOT, C.H., & HAMMOND, E.A. *The medical practitioners in medieval England: a biographical register.* Wellcome Historical Medical Library, 1965.

RAACH, JOHN H. *A directory of English country physicians, 1603-1643.* Dawsons of Pall Mall, 1962. List with brief notes.

WALLIS, J., & WALLIS, R.V. *Eighteenth century medics (subscriptions, licences, apprenticeships).* 2nd ed. Newcastle Upon Tyne: Project for Historical Bibliography, 1988. Over 35,000 names listed, with dates, places, etc.

WALLIS, PETER, & WALLIS, RUTH. 'Eighteenth century medics: the P.H.I.B.B. collective biography', in ROLLS, ROGER, GUY, JEAN, & GUY, JOHN, eds. *A pox on the provinces: proceedings of the 12th Congress of the British Society for the History of Medicine.* Bath: Bath University Press, 1990, 129-39.

The medical register for the year 1779. [ ], 1779. Reprinted on 5 fiche, Society of Genealogists, 1990.

The British medical directory for England, Scotland and Wales. The Lancet, 1853-4. 2 issues. Extensive listing; includes brief obituaries. Described as the 'antidote' to the 'poison' of the *London & Provincial directory!'*

LARA, B.W. *The medical list, or, English medical directory for 1857, being a register of the names and addresses of all qualified gentlemen actually practising the science of medicine ...* Lane and Lara, 1857.

PHILLIMORE, W.P.W. *Dictionary of medical specialists, being a classified list of London practitioners who chiefly attend to special departments of medicine and surgery, with particulars of the principal special hospitals and special departments in general hospitals.* Chas. J.Clark, 1889.

Medical and dental students' register: lists of medical and dental students registered during the year 1937. Constable & Co., for the General Medical Council, 1937.

GENERAL MEDICAL COUNCIL. *Register of medical students and dental students admitted to schools of medicine and to schools of dentistry in the academical year 1938-39.* Constable & Co., for the General Medical Council, [1939].

The medical directory, 18--, including the London medical directory, the Provincial Medical directory, the Medical directory for Wales, the Medical directory for Scotland, the Medical directory for Ireland. Churchill,

1845- . Annual; title varies. Originally published as *The London medical directory* and then as *The London and provincial medical directory*. Lists doctors, with notes on qualifications and appointments.

The medical register: pursuant to an act ... to regulate the qualifications of practitioners in medicine and surgery. General Medical Council, 1859- . Sub-title varies.

MONRO, THOMAS KIRKPATRICK. *The physician as man of letters, science and action.* 2nd ed. Edinburgh: E. & S. Livingstone, 1951. Contains many biographical notices of medical men active in other fields, e.g., diplomats, clergy, scientists, pirates, *etc.*

An important medical archive is described in:

SHEPPARD, JULIA. *Guide to The Contemporary Medical Archives Centre in the Wellcome Institute for the History of Medicine.* The Institute, 1971. Includes some biographical notes.

There are various biographical lists, *etc.,* of the members of particular medical colleges and institutions; these include:

Army Medical Services

PETERKIN, A., JOHNSTON, WILLIAM, & DREW, ROBERT, SIR. *Commissioned officers in the medical services of the British army, 1660-1960.* 2 vols. Wellcome Historical Medical Library, 1968. 1st vol originally published as two separate works: PETERKIN, ALFRED. *A list of commissioned medical officers of the army, Charles II to accession of George II.* Aberdeen: Aberdeen U.P., 1925, and JOHNSTON, WILLIAM. *Roll of commissioned officers in the Medical Service of the British army ... 1727 to ... 1898 ...* Aberdeen: Aberdeen U.P., 1917.

Guys Hospital

Directory of Guy's men (medical and dental), incorporating life members of the Clubs' Union. Ash & Co., 1922- . Annual; lists men nation-wide.

Royal College of Obstetricians and Gynaecologists

PEEL, JOHN, SIR. *The lives of the fellows of the Royal College of Obstetricians and Gynaecologists, 1929-1969.* William Heinemann Medical Books, 1976.

Royal College of Physicians

MUNK, WILLIAM. *The roll of the Royal College of Physicians of London, comprising biographical sketches of all the eminent physicians whose names are recorded in the annals from ... 1518 to ... 1825.* 2nd ed. 3 vols. Harrison & Sons, 1878.

This is continued by:

BROWN, G.H. *Lives of the fellows of the Royal College of Physicians of London, 1826-1925.* The College, 1955. Sometimes referred to as Munk's *Roll ...,* vol. 4. Further supplements have been edited by Richard R. Trail, to 1965, and Gordon Wolstenholme, to 1975 and 1983.

See also:

WOLSTENHOLME, GORDON, ed. *The Royal College of Physicians of London: portraits.* J. & A. Churchill, 1964. Listing of the College's portrait collection, with biographical notices on those portrayed.

Royal College of Surgeons

BAILEY, JAMES BLAKE. *List of officers and those who have obtained prizes at the Royal College of Surgeons of England, 1800-1895.* Taylor and Francis, 1896.

COPE, ZACAHRY. *The Royal College of Surgeons of England: a history.* Anthony Blond, 1959. Includes short biographies of leading surgeons, plus lists of presidents and members of council from 1800.

LE FANU, R. 'The archives of the College and its predecessor, the Company of Surgeons', *Annals of the Royal College of Surgeons of England* 12(4), 1953, 282-5. Brief description.

PLARR, VICTOR GUSTAVE. *Plarr's lives of the fellows of The Royal College of Surgeons of England* revised by Sir D'Arcy Power, Walter George Spencer, & George Ernest Gask. 2 vols. Bristol: J. Wright & Sons, for the Royal College of Surgeons, 1930. Continued by:

POWER, D'ARCY, SIR. *Lives of the fellows of the Royal College of Surgeons of England, 1930-1951.* The College, 1953.

ROYAL COLLEGE OF SURGEONS. *List of the members, fellows and licentiates in midwifery of the Royal College of Surgeons.* The College, 1825-64. Continued by:

ROYAL COLLEGE OF SURGEONS OF ENGLAND. *List of the fellows and members ...* The College, 1865-1965.

University of Leyden

SMITH, ROBERT WILLIAM INNES. *English speaking students of medicine at the University of Leyden.* Edinburgh: Oliver & Boyd, 1932. Biographical dictionary, with brief notes, listing 2,500 students.
See also Midwives, Naturopaths, and Nurses

Members of Parliament
See Parliamentarians

Merchant Seamen
See Seamen (Mercantile Marine)

Merchants

BOND, EDWARD A. 'Extracts from the liberate rolls, relative to loans supplied by Italian merchants to the Kings of England in the 13th and 14th centuries', *Archaeologia* **28**, 1840, 207-326. Includes many merchants' names.

BOURNE, H. R. FOX. *English merchants: memoirs in illustration of the progress of British commerce.* New ed. Chatto & Windus, 1898. Biographical essays on some 30 merchants.

ELMHIRST, EDWARD MARS. *Merchant marks,* ed. Leslie Dow. Harleian Society Publications, **108**. The Society, 1959. Gives names, towns, and dates.

RABB, THEODORE K. *Enterprise and empire: merchant and gentry investment in the expansion of England, 1575-1630.* Cambridge, Massachusetts: Harvard University Press, 1967. Includes index to 6336 persons involved in trade, colonization, and discovery, *etc.*
See also East India Men, Seamen (Mercantile Marine), and Tradesmen

Metal Trades
See Builders and Engineers

Metallurgists
See Mining Personnel

Midwives

AVELING, J.H. *English midwives: their history and prospects.* J.& A. Churchill, 1872. Mainly brief biographies.

Practising midwives and maternity nurses 1923-24: a classified directory alphabetically arranged. Scientific Press, 1923.
See also Medical Men

Millenialists

CAPP, B.S. *The fifth monarchy men: a study in seventeenth century millenarianism.* Faber & Faber, 1972. Includes a biographical dictionary.

Millers

STANLEY-MORGAN, R. 'Records of village mills', *Amateur historian* **2**(6), 1955, 172-4. Brief discussion of sources.

Millionaires

RUBINSTEIN, W.D. 'British millionaires, 1809-1949', *Bulletin of the Institute of Historical Research* **47**(116), 1974, 202-23. List based on probate records.

Miners
See Colliers and Mining personnel

Miniaturists
See Artists

Mining Personnel

REEKS, MARGARET. *Register of the associates and old students of the Royal School of Mines, and history of the Royal School of Mines.* Royal School of Mines (Old Students) Association, 1920.

The mining guide, containing the particulars of each mine, British and foreign: its situation, produce and officials, forming a complete mining directory. Mining Journal, 1853.

The mining year book: the busy man's book on mines, with directories of directors, secretaries, mining engineers and metallurgists ... Financial Times, 1901-12.

Who's who in mining and metallurgy. Mining Journal, 1908.
See also Colliers

Ministers of the Crown

HAZLEHURST, CAMERON, &WOODLAND, CHRISTINE. *A guide to the papers of British cabinet ministers, 1900-1951.* Guides & handbooks supplementary series, 1. Royal Historical Society, 1974. Includes biographical notes.

HISTORICAL MANUSCRIPTS COMMISSION. *Papers of British cabinet ministers, 1782-1900.* Guides to sources of British history, 1. H.M.S.O., 1982. Lists papers of over 200 ministers.

Ministers of the Crown *continued*

PICKRILL, D.A. *Ministers of the Crown.*
Routledge & Kegan Paul, 1981. Lists ministers
from the earliest known dates.
See also Politicians and Prime Ministers

Minstrels

BULLOCK-DAVIES, CONSTANCE. *Register of
royal and baronial domestic minstrels, 1272-
1327.* Woodbridge: Boydell Press, 1986. List,
with notes.
BULLOCK-DAVIES, CONSTANCE. *Menestrellorum
multitudo: minstrels at a royal feast.* Cardiff:
University of Wales Press, 1978. Includes
biographical notes on early 14th c.
minstrels.

Missing Persons

CHAPMAN, COLIN. 'The Central Tracing Agency
of the International Red Cross', *Family tree
magazine* **10**(7), 1994, 21-2. Traces persons
missing in conflicts.
*British Red Cross and Order of St. John
enquiry list no.14, 1917, wounded and
missing, containing all enquiries up to and
including July 20th 1917.* British Red Cross;
Order of St. John, 1917. Reprinted Newport:
Sunset Militaria, 1989.
*Enquiry list no.21, 1918: wounded and missing,
containing all enquiries up to and including
November 20th 1918.* British Red Cross;
Order of St. John, 1918. Lists 25,000
personnel reported missing.

Missionaries

COBB, HENRY S. 'The archives of the Church
Missionary Society', *Archives* **2**(14), 1955,
293-9.
KEEN, ROSEMARY. *A survey of the archives of
selected missionary societies.* Historical
Manuscripts Commission, 1968.
SIBREE, JAMES. *London Missionary Society: a
register of missionaries, deputations, etc.,
from 1796 to 1923.* London Missionary
Society, 1923. Biographical notes on 1,482
missionaries.

Money Lenders

*Grimstone's directory of persons registered to
lend money under the Moneylenders Act,
1900, during the 3½ years ending December
1912.* Alfred Grimstone, [1913].

Monks and Religious Orders

KNOWLES, DAVID,BROOKE, C.N.L., &LONDON, VERA
C.M. *The heads of religious houses in England
and Wales, 940-1216.* Cambridge: C.U.P., 1972.
Includes biographical notes with references to
sources.
DEVON, F. 'Inventory of the original
acknowledgements of the royal supremacy
made by religious houses &c., and deposited in
the Treasury of the Receipt of the Exchequer,
temp. Hen. VIII', *Seventh report of the Deputy
Keeper of the Public Records.* H.M.S.O., 1846,
279-306. Lists monks who took the oath of
supremacy, 1534.
HUNTER, JOSEPH. 'A catalogue of the deeds of
surrender of certain abbeys, priories, colleges,
hospitals, free chapels, chantries, bishopricks,
prebends and rectories, made in the reign of
King Henry the Eighth, with a few of the
reign of King Edward the Sixth, preserved
apart from the other records of the abolished
Court of Augmentations ...', *Eighth report of
the Deputy Keeper of the Public Records,*
1847, 37-51. Lists monks who signed surrenders.

Benedictines

SNOW, T.B. *Obit book of the English
Benedictines from 1600 to 1912, being the
necrology of the English Congregation of the
Order of St. Benedict from 1600 to 1883,*
revised by Henry Norbert Birt. Edinburgh:
J.C.Thomson, 1913.

Dominicans

CONWAY, J. PLACID, &JARRETT, BEDE, eds. *Lives
of the brethren of the order of preachers,
1206-1259.* Burns, Oates & Washbourne, 1924.
EMDEN, ALFRED B. *A survey of Dominicans in
England, based on the ordination lists in
episcopal registers, (1268-1538).* Dissertationes
historicae, fasciculus **18.** Rome: Institutum
Historicum Fratrum Praedicatorum, 1967.
Includes brief biographical notes.
GUMBLEY, WALTER. *Obituary notices of the
English Dominicans from 1555 to 1952.*
Blackfriars Publications, 1955. Biographies of
328 Dominican fathers.

Jesuits

EDWARDS, FRANCIS O. 'The archives of the
English Province of the Society of Jesus at
Farm Street, London', *Journal of the Society
of Archivists* **3**, 1965-9, 107-15.

EDWARDS, FRANCIS O. 'The archives of the English Province of the Society of Jesus', *Catholic archives* **1**, 1981, 20-25; **2**, 1982, 37-45.

FOLEY, HENRY. *Records of the English Province of the Society of Jesus: historic facts illustrative of the labours and sufferings of its members in the sixteenth and seventeenth centuries.* 7 vols. in 8. Burns & Oates, 1877-83. Includes much biographical information.

HOLT, GEOFFREY. *The English Jesuits, 1650-1829: a biographical dictionary.* Catholic Record Society publications (record series) **70.** 1984.

MCCOOG, THOMAS M. *English and Welsh Jesuits, 1555-1650.* Catholic Record Society publications (records series) **74.** 1994. Pt.1. A-F. To be continued.

See also Nuns

Motor Trades

PETERS, PERCY, &RUTTER, H.THORNTON. *Who's who in the motor trade: a biography, alphabetically arranged, of well-known members of the motor trade and prominent motorists.* Motor Commerce, 1934.

Who's who in the motor industry: a biographical dictionary. 14 vols. Grimsby: Roland C. Bellamy Publications, 1952-72. Title and publisher varies.

Motorists

RIDEN, PHILIP. *How to trace the history of your car: a guide to motor vehicle registration records in Great Britain, Ireland, the Isle of Man and Channel Islands.* Academy Books, 1991. Lists locations of car registration records.

See also Motor Trades

Mountaineers

MUMM, A.L. *The Alpine Club register, 1857-1863.* E.Arnold & Co., 1923. Biographical dictionary of mountaineers. Further vols. cover 1864-76 and 1877-90.

Murderers

LANE, BRIAN. *The Murder Club guide to South-West England and Wales.* Harrap, 1989. Guide to murderers and their victims, 12-20th c.

WILSON, PATRICK. *Murderess: a study of the women executed in Britain since 1843.* Michael Joseph, 1971. Detailed accounts of 68 trials.

Musicians

ASHBEE, ANDREW, ed. *Biographical dictionary of English court musicians, 1485-1714.* Forthcoming in 1996.

BROWN, JAMES D., & STRATTON, STEPHEN S. *British musical biography: a dictionary of musical artists, authors, and composers, born in Britain and its colonies.* Birmingham: S.S. Stratton, 1897. Brief biographies, mostly 19th c.

DE LAFONTAINE, HENRY CART, ed. *The King's musick: a transcript of records relating to music and musicians, 1460-1770.* New York: Da Capa Press, 1973. Originally published London, 1909. Includes biographical notes on many musicians.

The dramatic and musical directory of the United Kingdom. C.H. Fox, 1883-93. Annual? Lists singers, actors, musicians, etc.

HARLEY, JOHN. *British harpsichord music.* 2 vols. Aldershot: Scolar Press, 1992. v.1. Sources. v.2. History. Includes lists of composers, with extensive bibliography.

INCORPORATED SOCIETY OF MUSICIANS. *Handbook and register of members.* 1898- . Title varies.

MACKERNESS, E.D. 'Sources of local musical history', *Local historian* **11**, 1974-75, 315-20. Mentions some potential sources of biographical information.

The musical directory, annual and almanack. Rudall, Carte & Co., 1855-1931. Title varies. Alphabetical list of professions, music sellers, songs etc.

POPKIN, J.M. *Musical monuments.* K.G.Saur, 1986. Lists memorials to musicians, by place.

PULVER, JEFFREY A. *A biographical dictionary of old English music.* Kegan Paul, Trench, Trübner & Co., 1927.

SADIE, STANLEY, ed. *The new Grove dictionary of music and musicians.* 20 vols. Macmillan, 1980. The standard work.

SCHOLES, PERCY A. *The Oxford companion to music.* 10th ed. Oxford University Press, 1970.

Muscians *continued*

WYNDHAM, H.SAXE, & L'EPINE, GEOFFREY. *Who's who in music: a biographical record of contemporary musicians.* Sir Isaac Pitman & Sons, 1913-15. 2 editions.

Who's who in music and musicians international directory. Burke's Peerage, 1935-77. 8 editions. Publisher varies.

Original source material on musicians is found in two works by Ashbee:

ASHBEE, ANDREW. *Lists of payments to the King's musick in the reign of Charles II (1660-1685).* Snodland: A.Ashbee, 1981. Lists of names found in various accounts.

ASHBEE, ANDREW, ed. *Records of English court music.* 8 vols to date. Snodland: A.Ashbee; Aldershot: Scolar Press, 1986-93. v.1. 1660-1685. v.2. 1685-1714; v.3. 1625-1649; v.4.1603-1625; v.5.1625-1714; v.6.1558-1603; v.8. 1485-1558. Transcripts of the Lord Chancellors' records, with many names.

See also Actors, Minstrels, and Organists

Music Publishers
See Booksellers

Naturalists

RAVEN, CHARLES E. *English naturalists: from Neckham to Ray: a study of the modern world.* Cambridge: C.U.P., 1947. Biographies of leading naturalists.

Naturopaths

Directory of health practitioners: professional naturopaths, osteopaths, chiropractors, botano-therapists, biochemists, psychotherapists, etc. Croydon: [ ], 1935.

Naval Administrators

COLLINGE, J.M. *Navy Board officials, 1660-1832.* Office-holders in modern Britain, 7. Institute of Historical Research, 1978.

JACKSON, GEORGE, SIR. *Naval commissioners from 12 Charles II to I George III, 1660-1760: compiled from the original warrants and returns.* Lewes: the author, 1889. Includes brief biographies.

SAINTY, J.C. *Admiralty officials, 1660-1870.* Office-holders in modern Britain, 4. Athlone Press, 1975.

BRIGGS, JOHN HENRY, SIR. *Naval administrators, 1827 to 1892: the experience of 65 years,* ed. Lady Briggs. S. Low, Marston & Co., 1897. Alphabetical list of office-holders and events.

Naval Architects

INSTITUTION OF NAVAL ARCHITECTS. *List of members* ... The Institution, 1939- . Irregular. Now the 'Royal' Institution of Naval Architects.

Navy Agents

GREEN, GEOFFREY. 'Anglo-Jewish trading connections with officers and seamen of the Royal Navy, 1740-1820' *Jewish historical studies* **29**, 1982-6, 97-133. Includes a 'register of Jewish navy agents'.

Nonjurors

See Clergy and Landowners

Notaries Public

CHENEY, C.R. *Notaries public in England in the thirteenth and fourteenth centuries.* Oxford: Clarendon Press, 1972. Historical acount.

BROOKS, C.W., HELMHOLZ, R.H., & STEIN, P.G. *Notaries public in England since the Reformation.* Norwich: The Erskine Press for the Society of Public Notaries of London, 1991. General history.

PURVIS, J.S. 'The notary public in England', *Archivum* **12**, 1962, 121-6.

See also Lawyers

Nuisance Inspectors

MAYBREY, PATRICIA. 'Old occupations: the inspector of nuisances', *Family tree magazine* 11(4), 1995, 9-10.

Nuns

GANDY, MICHAEL. 'An index of nuns, 1598-1914', *Catholic ancestor* **4**(1), 1992, 14-18. Description of an index.

O'BRIEN, SUSAN. '10,000 nuns: working in convent archives', *Catholic archives* **9**, 1989, 26-33. Discussion of the author's research on nuns.

TRAPPES-LOMAX, RICHARD, ed. *The English Franciscan nuns, 1619-1821, and the Friars Minor of the same province, 1618-1761.* Publications of the Catholic Record Society **24**. 1922.

Nurse Children

CLARK, GILLIAN. 'Nurse-children: an unexpected source of family history', *Genealogists' magazine* 21(9), 1985, 319-20. A list of nurse children was being compiled to be lodged at the Society of Genealogists.

Nursemaids

CLARK, GILLIAN. 'London nurse children: a source of female employment in the rural domestic economy between 1540 and 1750', *Genealogists' magazine* 23(3), 1989, 97-101. General discussion of sources for women who fostered children in the Home Counties.

Nurserymen

See Horticulturalists

Nurses

ROSE, JANET R. 'Tracing your nurse ancestors', *Family tree magazine* 9(1), 1992, 21.

BURDETT, H., SIR. *Burdett's official nursing directory, 18--, containing ... a directory of nurses.* Scientific Press, 1898-1903. Annual.

GRAY, SHEILA. *The South African War, 1899-1902: service records of British and colonial women: a record of the service in South Africa of military and civilian nurses, laywomen and civilians.* Auckland: the author, 1993. Gives service records of over 1700 nurses.

The visiting nurses directory: London and county suburbs, provincial, Scotland, Wales. Scientific Press, 1923.

GENERAL NURSING COUNCIL FOR ENGLAND AND WALES. *The register of nurses ...* General Nursing Council, 1922- .

GENERAL NURSING COUNCIL FOR ENGLAND AND WALES. *The roll of assistant nurses, printed and published under the direction of the General Nursing Council of England and Wales in pursuance of the Nurses Act 1943, containing the names, qualifications, and addresses of assistant nurses enrolled under the Nurses Act, 1943. 1947-8 ...* General Nursing Council, 1947. Includes list of names removed from the roll, 1945-7.

GENERAL NURSING COUNCIL FOR ENGLAND AND WALES. *Names, qualifications and addresses of assistant nurses enrolled under the Nurses Act 1943, from 1st May 1948 to 31 August 1949, and names deleted from the roll since the publication of the 1948 edition.* General Nursing Council, [1949].

GENERAL NURSING COUNCIL FOR ENGLAND AND WALES. *List of persons admitted to or re-included in the roll of assistant nurses maintained by the General Nursing Council of England and Wales during the period ... together with names of persons ... removed from the roll during the same period.* The Council, 1950-67.

See also Midwives

Oarsmen

STEWARD, HERBERT THOMAS. *The records of Henley Royal Regatta from its institution in 1839 to 1902.* Grant Richards, 1903.

Opticians

JOINT COUNCIL OF QUALIFIED OPTICIANS. *The official register of qualified opticians ...* Joint Council of Qaulified Opticians, 1924-41. Annual.

Order of the British Empire

THORPE, A.WINTON, ed. *Burke's handbook to the most excellent Order of the British Empire, containing biographies, a full list of persons appointed to the order, showing their relative precedence, and coloured plates of the insignia.* Burke Publishing Co., 1921.

Organists and Organ Builders

Dictionary of organs and organists. 2nd ed. Geo. Aug. Mate & Son, 1921. Includes FREEMAN, ANDREW. 'Records of British organ builders, 940-1660'; also 'Organists who's who', *etc.*

LANGWILL, LYNDESAY G., & BOSTON, NOEL. *Church and chamber barrel-organs: their origin, makers, music and location: a chapter in English church music.* 2nd ed. Edinburgh: L.G.Langwill, 1970. Includes brief biographies of makers.

SHAW, WATKINS. *The succession of organists of the Chapel Royal and the cathedrals of England and Wales from c.1538; also of the organists of the collegiate churches of Westminster, certain academic foundations, and the cathedrals of Armagh and Dublin.* Oxford: Clarendon Press, 1991. Detailed biographical notes.

Organists and Organ Builders *continued*

WEST, JOHN EBENEZER. *Cathedral organists past and present: a record of the succession of organists of the cathedrals, chapels royal, and principal collegiate churches of the United Kingdom, from about the period of the Reformation until the present day, with biographical notes, extracts from the chapter books, anecdotes, &c.* Novello & Co., 1899.

Ornithologists

MULLENS, W.H., &SWANN, H. KIRKE. *A bibliography of British ornithology from the earliest times to the end of 1912, including biographical accounts of the principal writers and bibliographies of their published works.* Macmillan, 1917.

Orphans

CROSS, AVRIL. 'Dr. Barnardo's archives', *Family tree magazine* 11(10), 1995, 46-7.

KIRKHAM, JOHN. 'Barnardo's photographic and film archives', *Local history magazine* 41, 1993, 10-12. Discussion of the archive, which includes photographs of all Barnardo children.

Osteopaths

See Naturopaths

Painters

See Artists

Papermakers

SHORTER, ALFRED H. *Paper mills and paper makers in England, 1495-1800.* Monumenta chartae papyraceae historiam illustranti 6. Hilversum, Holland: Paper Publications Society, 1957. Topographical listing of mills and millers.

STIRK, JEAN. 'The paper makers', *Family tree magazine* 6(6), 1990, 4-5; 6(7), 1990, 4-5, & 6(8), 1990, 4-5.

Directory of paper makers of the United Kingdom. Marchant Singer and Co., 1877- . Annual. Title varies; issued with the *Paper makers monthly journal.*

Parliamentarians

Members of Parliament are perhaps more studied than any other occupation. For a detailed list of 984 studies of constituencies and their members, see:

SEATON, JANET. *English constituency histories, 1265-1832: a guide to printed sources.* House of Commons Library document 15. H.M.S.O., 1986.

A full list of M.Ps to 1874 is provided by:

Return of the names of every member of the lower house of the Parliaments of England, Scotland and Ireland, with name of constituency represented and date of return, 1213-1874. 3 vols. House of Commons papers, 1878, **LXII,** pts. 1-3. H.M.S.O., 1878. See also 1890-1, vol. **LXII,** for continuation to 1885.

Many biographical dictionaries of M.P.s are available:

WEDGWOOD, JOSIAH C., & HOLT, ANNE D. *History of Parliament: biographies of the members of the Commons house, 1439-1509.* H.M.S.O., 1936. See also the same authors' *History of Parliament: register of the ministers and of the members of both houses, 1439-1509.* H.M.S.O., 1938.

BINDOFF, S.T. *The House of Commons, 1509-1558.* 3 vols. Secker & Warburg, 1982.

HASLER, W. *The House of Commons, 1558-1603.* 3 vols. H.M.S.O., 1981.

'The Parliament of 1614', *Palatine note-book* 3, 1883, 125-31. Lists M.Ps.

KEELER, MARY FREAR. *The Long Parliament, 1640-1641: a biographical study of its members.* Philadelphia: American Philosophical Society, 1954.

HENNING, BASIL DUKE. *The House of Commons, 1660-90.* 3 vols. Secker & Warburg, 1983.

CHERRY, GEORGE L. *The Convention Parliament, 1689: a biographical study of its members.* New York: Bookman Associates, 1966. Biographical dictionary.

SEDGEWICK, ROMNEY. *The House of Commons, 1715-1754.* 3 vols. H.M.S.O., 1970.

JUDD, GERRIT. *Members of Parliament, 1734-1832.* New Haven: Yale University Press, 1955. Includes checklist of 5,034 M.P.'s.

NAMIER, LEWIS, SIR, & BROOKE, JOHN. *The House of Commons, 1754-1790.* 3 vols. H.M.S.O., 1964.

THORNE, R.G. *The House of Commons, 1790-1820.* 5 vols. Secker & Warburg, 1986.

STENTON, MICHAEL, et al. *Who's who of British members of parliament: a biographical dictionary of the House of Commons.* 4 vols. Hassocks, Sussex: Harvester Press, 1976-81. Vol.1. 1832-85. Vol.2. 1886-1918. Vol.3. 1919-45. Vol.4. 1945-79.

Dod's Parliamentary companion. Whitaker, 1832- . Annual. Title varies. Includes M.P.s biographies.

Vacher's parliamentary companion, containing lists of the House of Lords and House of Commons, with members' town addresses. A.S. Kerswill, 1832- . Quarterly.

Debretts House of Commons and the judicial bench. Dean & Sons, 1867-1931. Includes biographies of county court judges, recorders, stipendiary magistrates, Scots, Irish and colonial judges.

THE TIMES. *The new House of Commons.* The Times, 1880- . Issued after almost every general election. Became *The Times House of Commons* from 1910- . Includes brief biographies.

HUMBERSTONE, THOMAS LORD. *University representation.* Hutchinson & Co., 1951. Includes a biographical index of the M.P.s for the universities of Oxford, Cambridge, Dublin, London, *etc.*

See also Ministers of the Crown and Politicians

Parliamentary Officers

MARSDEN, PHILIP. *The officers of the Commons, 1363-1978.* H.M.S.O., 1979. Appendices provides lists of speakers, clerks & sergeants at arms.

MCKAY, W.R. *Clerks in the House of Commons, 1363-1989: a biographical list.* House of Lords Record Office occasional publications, **3.** H.M.S.O., 1989.

MCKAY, W.R. *Secretaries to Mr. Speaker.* House of Commons Library document **14.** H.M.S.O., 1086. Includes list from 1606.

SAINTY, J.C. *Officers of the House of Lords, 1485 to 1971: a list.* Memorandum, **45.** House of Lords Record Office, 1971.

SAINTY, J.C. *The Parliament Office in the seventeenth and eighteenth centuries: biographical notes on clerks in the House of Lords, 1600-1800.* House of Lords Record Office, 1977.

SAINTY, JOHN, SIR. *The Parliament Office in the nineteenth and early twentieth centuries: biographical notes on clerks in the House of Lords, 1800 to 1939.* House of Lords Record Office, 1990.

THORNE, PETER. *Sergeant for the Commons.* House of Commons Library document **13.** H.M.S.O., 1985. Includes list from 1415.

See also Chaplains

Passengers (Titanic)

EATON, JOHN P., &HAAS, CHARLES A. *Titanic: triumph and tragedy.* 2nd ed. Sparkford: Patrick Stephens, 1994. Includes passenger list.

Titanic disaster: report of the Committee on Commerce, United States Senate, pursuant to S.Res.283, directing the Committee on Commerce to investigate the causes leading to the wreck of the White Star liner Titanic ... 62nd Congress, 2nd session, Senate Report **806.** Washington: Government Printing Office, 1912. Includes list of passengers and crew.

See also Seamen (Mercantile Marine)

Patent Agents

CHARTERED INSTITUTE OF PATENT AGENTS. *Register of patent agents.* The Institute, 1889- .

Patentees

SMITH, BARBARA M.D. 'Patents for invention: the national and local picture', *Business history* 4(2), 1962, 109-19. General discussion of sources.

PALGRAVE, FRANCIS. 'Calendar of specifications enrolled upon the Close Rolls', *Sixth report of the Deputy Keeper of the Public Records.* H.M.S.O., 1845, 155-203; *Seventh report* ... 1846, 188-210. Lists applicants for patents, 1712-1810. No index.

'Patents and the family historian', *Manchester genealogist* **25**(4), 1989, 11-13. Brief note.

See also Inventors

Patrons (Ecclesiastical)

[GILBERT, RICHARD]. *Patroni ecclesiarum, or, a list of the patrons of the dignities, rectories, vicarages, perpetual curacies, chapelries, endowed lectureships, &c., of the united church of England and Ireland, with the valuation annexed of all livings not exceeding £150 per annum, as returned.* C.G.J. & F. Rivington, 1831. Issued as a supplement to the *Clerical guide.*

Pawnbrokers

PRICE, F. G. HILTON. 'Some notes upon the signs of the pawnbrokers in London in the seventeenth and eighteenth centuries', *Archaeological journal* **59**, 1902, 160-200. Includes list of pawnbrokers.

Pedlars
See Chapmen

Pewterers
COTTERELL, HOWARD HERSCHEL. *Old pewter: its makers and marks in England, Scotland and Ireland: an account of the old pewterer and his craft.* B.T.Batsford, 1929. Reprinted 1968. Includes an extensive 'alphabetical list of pewterers'.

JACKSON, RADWAY. *English pewter touchmarks, including the marks of origin of some of the Scottish and Irish pewterers,* ed. Ronald F. Michaelis. W.Foulsham & Co., 1970.

Pharmacists
The registers of pharmaceutical chemists and chemists and druggists. Pharmaceutical Society of Great Britain, 1869- . Title varies. Alphabetical lists by name, giving residence, qualifications, etc.

Photographers
MATTHEWS, RUTH. *Who's who in photography.* Focal Press, 1951.

ROYAL PHOTOGRAPHIC SOCIETY OF GREAT BRITAIN. *List of members of the Royal Photographic Society.* The Society, 1895-1942. Irregular.

Physiologists
O'CONNOR, W.J. *British physiologists, 1885-1914: a biographical dictionary.* Manchester: Manchester University Press, 1991.

Pig Breeders
The pig-breeder's who's who for 1925. Organised Publicity, 1925.

Pilots
CHAPLIN, W.R. *The Corporation of Trinity House of Deptford Strond from the year 1660.* Cockayne & Co., 1950. Includes lists of masters, brethren, *etc.*

HARRIS, G.G. *The Trinity House of Deptford, 1514-1660.* Athlone Press, 1969. Includes brief lists of masters and brethren.

Pipemakers
BERRY, GEORGE. 'Seventeenth century tokens of pipe-makers, tobacconists, and other dealers in tobacco and pipes', in DAVEY, PETER, ed. *The archaeology of the clay tobacco pipe VII: more pipes and kilns from England.* B.A.R. British series **100**. Oxford: B.A.R., 1982, 355-76. Includes topographical listing.

DAVEY, PETER, ed. *The archaeology of the clay tobacco pipe, 1: Britain: the Midlands and Eastern England.* B.A.R.British series **63**. 1979. Includes many lists of pipemakers.

DAVEY, PETER, ed. *The archaeology of the clay tobacco pipe, 9: More pipes from the Midlands and Eastern England.* 2 vols. B.A.R.British series **146**. 1985.

HAMMOND, PETER J. 'Was your ancestor a pipemaker?' *Family tree magazine* **4**(10), 1988, 4-6.

OSWALD, ADRIAN. 'The archaeology and economic history of English clay tobacco pipes', *Journal of the British Archaeological Association* 3rd series, **22**, 1959, 40-102. Includes 48 page list of pipe makers, showing places and dates, with bibliography.

Pirates
GOSSE, PHILIP. *The pirate's who's who, giving particulars of the lives and deaths of the pirates and buccaneers.* Dulau & Co., 1924. Biographical dictionary.

Planemakers
GOODMAN, W.L. *British planemakers from 1700.* 2nd ed. Needham Market: Arnold & Walker, 1978. Includes 'check list of planemakers and dealers', and 'check list of plane-iron makers'.

Playwrights
See Actors, Musicians and Poets

Poets
SAUNDERS, J.W. *A biographical dictionary of Renaissance poets and dramatists, 1520-1650.* Brighton: Harvester Press, 1983.

Policemen
BRIDGEMAN, IAN, & EMSLEY, CLIVE. *Guide to the archives of the police forces of England and Wales.* Monograph 2. [ ]: Police History Society, 1991. Looseleaf.

PEARL, SUSAN. 'The policeman', *Family tree magazine* **6**(12), 1990, 25-7.

WATERS, LES. *Notes for family historians.* Police history monograph, 1. Police History Society, 1987.

The journal of the Police History Society,
The Society, 1986- .
The police and constabulary list 1844.
Monograph 3. Leigh on Sea: Police History
Society, 1990. Facsimile; originally
published as *A general police and
constabulary list and analysis of criminal
and police statistics ...* Parker, Furnivall and
Parker, 1844.

Politicians

GREAVES, RICHARD L., & ZALLER, ROBERT.
*Biographical dictionary of British radicals
in the seventeenth century.* 3 vols.
Brighton: Harvester Press, 1982-4.
BAYLEN, JOSEPH O. & GOSSMAN, NORBERT J.
*Biographical dictionary of modern British
radicals.* 4 vols. New York: Harvester Press,
1979-84. v.1. 1770-1830. v.2. 1830-1870. v.3.
1870-1914. v.4. 1915-1970.
COOK, CHRIS, et al. *Sources in British
political history, 1900-1951.* Macmillan,
1975- . Contents: v.1. A guide to the archives
of selected organisations and societies. v.2.
A guide to the private papers of selected
public servants. v.3-4. A guide to the private
papers of members of parliament. v.5. A
guide to the private papers of selected
writers, intellectuals and publicists. v.6.
First consolidated supplement. Vols. 2-5
include brief biographical notes.
HISTORICAL MANUSCRIPTS COMMISSON.
Papers of British politicians, 1782-1900.
Guides to sources for British history, 7.
H.M.S.O., 1989. Lists papers of 705
politicians.
See also Ministers of the Crown, Prime
Ministers, and Parliamentarians

Porcelain Manufacturers

GODDEN, GEOFFREY. *Encyclopaedia of British
porcelain manufacturers.* Barrie & Jenkins,
1988.
See also Potters and Silversmiths

Postmen

FARRUGIA, JEAN. *A guide to Post Office
archives.* Post Office, 1987. See especially
the list of staff records.
FARRUGIA, JEAN. 'The archives of the British
Post Office', *Family tree magazine* 22(8),
1995, 46-8.

PHILLIPS, ADRIAN. 'Post Office H.Q.'s Record
Office', *Greentrees: the journal of the
Central Middlesex Family History Society*
2(5), 1981, 8-9. Brief note.
PHILLIPS, ADRIAN. 'Post Office Headquarters'
Record Office', *The North Middlesex:
journal of the North Middlesex Family
History Society* 3(2), 1981, 30. Brief note.
SQUELCH, KEVIN. 'The archives of the British
Post Office', *Family history news and digest*
10(3), 1996, 126-8.
*List of the principal officers in the Post
Office, and particulars of the metropolitan
and provincial establishments and of British
post offices and agencies abroad.* H.M.S.O.,
1911. A further edition was published in
1936.

Potters

BREARS, PETER C.D. *The English country
pottery: its history and techniques.* Newton
Abbot: David & Charles, 1971. Many names
are mentioned in the gazetteer.
CHAFFERS, WILLIAM. *Marks and monograms
on European and oriental pottery and
porcelain, with historical notices of each
manufactory,* ed. Frederick Littlefield.
Reeves and Turner, 1932. Includes names of
numerous potters and porcelain
manufacturers.
FISHER, S.W. *English pottery and porcelain
marks, including Scottish and Irish marks.*
Slough: W. Foulsham & Co., 1970.
GODDEN, GEOFFREY A. *Encyclopaedia of
British pottery and porcelain marks.* Herbert
Jenkins, 1964.
GODDEN, GEOFFREY. *The handbook of British
pottery and porcelain marks.* Herbert
Jenkins, 1968. Reprinted Barrie and Jenkins,
1990. Includes list of manufacturers; also list
of 'Staffordshire potters of the 1780s'.
OSWALD, ADRIAN, et al. *English brown
stoneware, 1670-1900.* Faber & Faber, 1982.
Includes brief notes on many potters.
See also Silversmiths.

Prime Ministers

BROOKE, JOHN. *The Prime Minister's papers,
1801-1902: a survey of the privately
preserved papers of those statesmen who
held the office of Prime Minister during the
19th century.* H.M.S.O., 1968.

Printers
See Booksellers

Prisoners
See Criminals

Prisoners of State
'Index to the records in the custody of the
Constable of the Tower of London, relating
to the state prisoners, garrison, *etc.*',
*Thirteenth annual report of the Deputy
Keeper of the Public Records* 1869, appendix,
313-59. Includes index to prisoners of state.

Prisoners of War
ABELL, FRANCIS. *Prisoners of war in Britain,
1756 to 1815: a record of their lives, their
romance, and their sufferings.* Oxford
University Press, 1914. General study.
MARTIN, PAULA. *Spanish Armada prisoners: the
story of the Nuestra Senora del Rosario and
her crew, and of other prisoners in England,
1587-97.* Exeter maritime studies 1. Exeter:
University of Exeter, 1988. Includes list of
prisoners.
GASTON, PETER. *Korea 1950-1953 prisoners of
war: the British Army.* London Stamp
Exchange, [1976]. List.
*List of British officers taken prisoner in the
various theatres of war between August 1914
and November 1918.* Cox & Co., 1919.
Reprinted London Stamp Exchange, 1988.
*Prisoners of war: British Army 1939-1945:
alphabetical nominal registers (including
number, rank, P.O.W. number, regiment or
corps and camp location details) listing over
107,000 British Army prisoners of war of all
ranks held in Germany and German occupied
territories.* H.M.S.O., 1945. Reprinted
Polstead: J.B.Hayward & Son, 1990.
*Prisoners of war: naval and air forces of Great
Britain and the Empire, 1939-1945 ...*
H.M.S.O., 1945. Reprinted Polstead: J.B.
Hayward, 1990.
WALKER, T.J. *The Depot for prisoners of war at
Norman Cross, Huntingdonshire, 1796 to
1816.* 2nd ed. Constable & Co., 1915. Includes
an extensive list of British prisoners of war at
Verdun, 1804-14.

Psychotherapists
See Naturopaths

Publicans
JOHNSON, W.BRANCH. 'Some sources of inn
history', *Amateur historian* 6(1), 1963, 18-21.
Lists many sources potentially of
genealogical value.
TATE, W.E. 'Public house bibliography:
topographical guide to the histories of
English inns and inn-signs', *Local historian*
8, 1968-9, 126-30. Identifies many regional
works listing public houses, some of which
may include information on publicans.
*A complete coaching directory and packet
guide, giving information of all coaches,
packets or other conveyances.* C.W.Leonard,
[1850?] Useful for its list of coaching inns,
which gives names of innkeepers.
*The illustrated who's who of the licensing
trade: a directory of licensees and a guide to
specialist suppliers to the licensed trade and
its customers.* 4 vols. Current Trade Covers,
1950. Also 3 vols published 1952.

Publishers
See Booksellers

Puritans
GARRETT, CHRISTINA HALLOWELL. *The Marian
exiles: a study in the origins of Elizabethan
Puritanism.* Cambridge: Cambridge
University Press, 1938. Biographical
dictionary of 472 puritan exiles, from all
walks of life.

Radicals
See Politicians

Railwaymen
The standard guides to railway staff records
are:
HAWKINGS, DAVID. *Railway ancestors: a guide
to the staff records of the railway companies
of England and Wales, 1822-1947.* Alan
Sutton, 1995.
RICHARDS, TOM. *Was your grandfather a
railwayman? A directory of records relating
to staff employed by railways in the
following countries, with details of material
and repositories: United Kingdom, Australia,
Canada, Eire, India, New Zealand, United
States of America.* 3rd ed. Birmingham:
F.F.H.S. 1995.
See also:

FOWKES, E.H. 'Sources of history in railway records of British Transport Historical Records', *Journal of the Society of Archivists* **3**, 1965-9, 476-88. Now somewhat out of date.

HARDY, FRANK. 'Railway records for the family historian', *Genealogists' magazine* **23**(7), 1990, 256-60. Useful general discussion.

OTTLEY, GEORGE. *A bibliography of British railway history.* 2nd ed. H.M.S.O., 1983. Supplement published 1988. Useful for general background information, but, apart from a few biographies, includes little of direct genealogical value.

OTTLEY, GEORGE. *Railway history: a guide to sixty one collections in libraries and archives in Great Britain.* Birmingham: Library Association Reference, Special and Information Section, 1973.

SIMMONS, JACK. 'Railway history in English local records', *Journal of transport history* **1**, 1953-4, 155-69. General discussion of records, including those relating to staff and shareholders.

Railway Engineers

MARSHALL, JOHN. *A biographical dictionary of railway engineers.* Newton Abbot: David & Charles, 1978. Includes 600 biographies.

Railway Officials and Shareholders

TUCK, H. *The railway directory for 1850, containing the names of the directors and principal officers of the railways in Great Britain and Ireland, derived from authentic sources.* Railway Times Office, 1850.

An alphabetical list of the names, descriptions, and places of abode of all persons subscribing to the amount of £2,000 and upwards to any railway subscription contract ... House of Commons papers, 1845, **40**. H.M.S.O., 1845. Extensive list of shareholders. The same volume also has lists of those subscribing under £2,000. For a similar list, see also House of Commons papers, 1846, **30**.

Bradshaw's railway manual, shareholders' guide and directory, 1869. Newton Abbot: David & Charles Reprints, 1969. Originally published W.J. Adams, 1869. Reprint of one volume of an annual published from 1848 to 1923, which lists directors and officials of each railway company.

Railway yearbook. Railway Publishing Co., 1898-1932. Includes a 'who's who' of the railway world.

Universal directory of railway officials. St.Margarets Technical Press, 1894-1949. Annual; publisher varies.

See also Railwaymen

Refugees (Huguenot)

SHAW, WILLIAM A. 'The English government and the relief of Protestant refugees', *Proceedings of the Huguenot Society of London* **5**, 1894-6, 343-42. Includes many extracts from King's warrant books, 17-18th c., giving names of refugee pensioners. Reference should also be made to Raymond's *English genealogy: a bibliography,* sections 14E and 17B.

See also Clergy (Huguenot)

Retainers

JONES, MICHAEL, & WALKER, SIMON, eds. 'Private indentures for life service in peace and war, 1278-1476', in *Camden miscellany* **32**. Camden 5th series **3**, 1994, 1-190.

LEWIS, N.B. ed. 'Indentures of retinue with John of Gaunt, Duke of Lancaster, enrolled in Chancery, 1367-1399', in *Camden miscellany* **22**. Camden 4th series **1**, 1964, 77-112.

WALKER, SIMON. *The Lancastrian affinity, 1361-1399.* Oxford: Clarendon Press, 1990. Includes list of retainers.

Ropemakers

See Fishmongers

Royal Marines

BLUMBERG, H.E. *Britain's sea soldiers: a record of the Royal Marines during the war 1914-1919.* Devonport: Swiss & Co., 1927. Includes various lists of names.

FRASER, EDWARD, & CARR-LAUGHTON, L.G. *The Royal Marine Artillery, 1804-1923.* 2 vols. Royal United Services Institution, 1930. v.1. 1804-1859. v.2. 1859-1923. Includes various lists of officers, *etc.*

THOMAS, GARTH. *Records of the Royal Marines.* P.R.O. readers' guide **10**. P.R.O. Publications, 1994.

Bid them rest in peace: a register of Royal Marine deaths, 1939-45. [ ]: Royal Marines Historical Society, 1992. Cover title.

Royal Marines *continued*

Royal Marines honours and awards, 1900-1970. London Stamp Exchange, [197-?]

With full and grateful hearts: a register of Royal Marines deaths, 1914-19. [ ]: Royal Marines Historical Society, 1992.

Royalist 'Delinquents'
See Landowners

Rugby Players
GODWIN, TERRY. *The complete who's who of international rugby.* Poole: Blandford Press, 1987. Predominantly British and Australian.

Sailmakers
See Fishmongers

Salt Merchants
See Fishmongers

Scientists
Archives of British men of science. Booklet and microfiche. Mansell, 1972. Data on 3,400 scientists, including citations to obituaries, and notes on location of papers.

HISTORICAL MANUSCRIPTS COMMISSON. *The manuscript papers of British scientists, 1600-1940.* Guides to sources for British history, **2.** H.M.S.O., 1982. Lists papers of 635 scientists.

HUNTER, MICHAEL. *The Royal Society and its fellows, 1660-1700: the morphology of an early scientific institution.* Chalfont St. Giles: British Society for the History of Science, 1982. Includes 'catalogue of fellows, 1660-1700', listing 551 names; also various other nominal lists.

RAISTRICK, ARTHUR. *Quakers in science and industry, being an account of the Quaker contributions to science and industry during the 17th and 18th centuries.* Newton Abbot: David & Charles, 1968.

Register of old students and staff of the Royal College of Science. 6th ed. Royal College of Science Association, 1951.

ROYAL SOCIETY OF LONDON. *Obituaries of deceased fellows chiefly for the period 1898-1904, with a general index to previous obituary notices.* Harrison & Sons, 1905.

ROYAL SOCIETY OF LONDON. *Obituary notices of fellows.* 9 vols. Royal Society of London, 1932-1954.

ROYAL SOCIETY OF LONDON. *Biographical memoirs of fellows of the Royal Society.* Royal Society, 1955- .

ROYAL SOCIETY OF LONDON. *The record of the Royal Society of London for the Promotion of Natural Knowledge.* 4th ed. The Society, 1940. Includes list of fellows, etc.

Sculptors
CHANCELLOR, E.BERESFORD. *The lives of the British sculptors and those who have worked in England from the earliest days to Sir Francis Chantrey.* Chapman & Hall, 1911. Prominent lives.

GRANT, MAURICE HAROLD. *A dictionary of British sculptors, from the XIIIth to the XXth century.* Rockliff, 1953.

GUNNIS, RUPERT. *Dictionary of British Sculptors, 1660-1851.* New rev. ed. Murrays, 1968.

See also Artists

Seamen (Mercantile Marine)
The standard guide to tracing merchant seamen is:

WATTS, C.T. *My ancestor was a merchant seaman: how can I find out more about him?* Rev. ed. Society of Genealogists, 1991.

See also:

TAYLOR, W.J. 'Notes on sources 14: 19th century seamen's records', *Lancashire [Rossendale Society for Genealogy and Heraldry journal]* 5(4), 1984, 27-31. Brief note.

WATTS, CHRISTOPHER T., & MICHAEL, J. 'Unravelling merchant seamen's records', *Genealogists' magazine* **19,** 1977-8, 313-21.

WOOD, TOM. 'Records of merchant seamen', *Family tree magazine* 7(6-7), 1991, *passim.*

JONES, A.G.E. 'John Biscoe: tracing a master mariner', *Local historian* 8(5), 160-66. Valuable account of sources used to trace a 19th c. explorer and seaman.

Some 500 libraries and record offices with maritime collections are listed in:

BRYON, RITA V., & BRYON, TERENCE N. *Maritime information: a guide to libraries and sources of information in the United Kingdom.* 3rd ed. Witherby and Co., for the Maritime Information Association, 1993. Includes brief appendices on crew lists and Royal Navy personnel records.

Seamen (Mercantile Marine) *continued*

A number of guides *etc.,* to the more important collections are available:

Lloyds Marine Collection

BARRISKILL, D.T. *A guide to the Lloyd's marine collection and related marine sources at Guildhall Library.* 2nd ed. Guildhall Library, 1994. Detailed guide to an important collection for seamen, 18-20th c.

'Lloyds marine collection', *Family History Society of Cheshire [journal]* 12(1), 1982, 4-5. Brief.

Maritime History Archive

THOMAS, ROBERTA. 'The Maritime History Archive: sources for research', *Family history news and digest* 9(3), 1994, 98-102. Includes discussion of 'crew agreements', 1863-92.

ALEXANDER, DAVID. 'A description of indexing procedures for the agreement on account of crew', *Archives* 11(50), 1973, 86-93. Discussion of an index to an extensive collection of 'crew agreements' held by the Maritime History Group of the Memorial University of Newfoundland.

Registrar-General of Shipping and Seamen

COX, NICHOLAS. 'The records of the Registrar-General of Shipping and Seamen', *Maritime history* 2, 1972, 168-88. Archival list, calendaring many items of interest, e.g. registers of births, deaths and marriages at sea, crew lists, apprenticeship records, *etc.*

STEPHENSON, B.C. *Lloyd's captains register, containing the names and services of certificated masters of the British mercantile marine now afloat, compiled from the records of the Registrar-General of Seamen ...* J.D.Potter, 1869.

Southampton

JOYE, GILL. *Catalogue of the maritime collection.* Southampton: Southampton Reference Library, 1981.

A catalogue of crew lists and ships' agreements, 1863-1913, in the Southampton City Record Office. Southampton: the Office, 1983. Cover title: *Southampton crew lists 1863-1913: a catalogue of the records.*

Wilson Line

'The Wilson Line Archive', *Paragon review: newsletter of the Division of Archives and Special Collections [Brynmor Jones Library, University of Hull]* 1, 1992, 4-7. The archive includes records of masters, officers, *etc.*

A useful source for identifying the names of ships' masters and merchants is dicussed in:
WOODWARD, DONALD. 'The port books of England and Wales', *Maritime history* 3, 1973, 147-65.

Census records for seamen are discussed in:
BURTON, V.C. 'A floating population: vessel enumeration returns in censuses, 1851-1921', *Local population studies* 38, 1987, 36-43.

Many articles likely to be of interest to those with seamen amongst their ancestors are printed in:
The mariner's mirror: the journal of the Society for Nautical Research. The Society, 1911- . An index is provided by ANDERSON, R.C. --"--: *general index to volumes 1-35.* Cambridge: C.U.P., 1955. Covers issues from 1911-1949.

The official list of seamen is:
The mercantile navy list. H.M.S.O., 1850- . Irregular, lists masters, mates, pilots, engineers, officers, etc.

Biographical notes on prominent seamen are given in:
UDEN, GRANT, & COOPER, RICHARD. *A dictionary of British ships and seamen.* Allen Lane/Kestrel Books, 1980.

For men from the lower deck, consult:
Trinity House petitions: a calendar of the records of the Corporation of Trinity House, London, in the library of the Society of Genealogists. Society of Genealogists, 1987. Amongst the functions of Trinity House was that of providing succour for distressed mariners. This calendar lists the names of those who petitioned for relief.

The study of medals awarded to seamen by Lloyds may be of value to genealogists. See:
GAWLER, JIM. *Lloyd's medals 1836-1989: a history of medals awarded by the Corporation of Lloyds.* Toronto: Harts Publishing, 1989.

BROWN, GEORGE A. *Lloyd's war medal for bravery at sea.* Langley, British Columbia: Western Canadian Distributors, 1992. Extracts from *Lloyds list and shipping gazette,* 1940-48.

Seamen (Mercantile Marine) *continued*
Many merchant seamen lost their lives in the
two world wars. Various rolls of honour and
lists of war graves are available; see:
IMPERIAL WAR GRAVES COMMISSION.
   *Introduction to the register of the Tower Hill
   memorial to those officers and men of the
   merchant navy and fishing fleets who fell in
   the Great War through enemy action and
   whose graves are not known.* The
   Commission, 1928. Reprinted with
   amendments Maidenhead: Commonwealth War
   Graves Commission, 1985.
IMPERIAL WAR GRAVES COMMISSION. *Register
   of the mercantile marine memorial, Tower
   Hill, London.* 8 pts. The Commission, 1928.
   Reprinted with amendments Maidenhead:
   Commonwealth War Graves Commission,
   1984-91.
IMPERIAL WAR GRAVES COMMISSION. *War dead
   of the British Commonwealth; the register of
   the names of those of the merchant navy and
   fishing fleet who fell in the 1939-1945 war
   and have no other grave than the sea: the
   Tower Hill memorial.* The Commission, 1955.
   Reprinted with amendments Maidenhead:
   Commonwealth War Graves Commission,
   1984-5.
MINISTRY OF TRANSPORT AND CIVIL AVIATION.
   *Roll of honour of the merchant navy and
   fishing fleets, 1939-1945.* 3 vols. The Ministry,
   [1955]. Lists 33,000 who lost their lives.
See also Boatmen, Seamen (Royal Navy), and
Shipowners

Seamen (Royal Navy)
The standard guide to Royal Navy personnel
records is now:
RODGER, N.A.M. *Naval records for genealogists.*
   Public Record Office handbooks, **22**. H.M.S.O.,
   1988.
For a brief general discussion of printed
sources, see:
HURST, NORMAN. 'Printed sources of naval
   biography and history', *Family tree magazine*
   4(11), 1988, 20.
Comprehensive listings of publications on the
Royal Navy are provided by:
MANWARING, GEORGE ERNEST. *A bibliography
   of British naval history: a biographical and
   historical guide to printed manuscript
   sources.* G. Routledge, 1930. Includes list of
   biographies.

NATIONAL MARITIME MUSEUM. *Catalogue of
   the library.* 5 vols in 8. H.M.S.O., 1968.
   Contents: v.1. Voyages and travel. v.2.
   Biography [includes many lists.] v.3. Atlases
   and cartography. v.4. Piracy and privateering.
   v.5. Naval history.
For the Second World War, see:
LAW, DEREK G. *The Royal Navy in World War
   Two: an annotated bibliography.* Greenhill
   Books, 1988.
The National Maritime Museum also possesses
extensive archival collections, which are listed
in:
KNIGHT, R.J.B. *Guide to the manuscripts in the
   National Maritime Museum.* 2 vols. Mansell,
   1977-90. Contents: v.1. The personal
   collections. v.2. Public Records, business
   records, and artificial collections.
Another important archival collection is
described in:
TANNER, J.R., ed. *A descriptive catalogue of
   the naval manuscripts in the Pepysian
   Library at Magdalene College, Cambridge.*
   3 vols. Publications **26, 27 & 36**. Navy
   Records Society, 1904-9. Vol. 1. includes
   various lists of officers, 1660-88.
For Admiralty records, see:
*List of Admiralty records preserved in the
   Public Record Office.* Public Record Office
   lists and indexes **18**. New York: Kraus
   Reprint, 1963. Vol.1. All published. The
   records listed include many lists *etc.*, of
   seamen and other personnel.
'Admiralty records as sources for biography
   and genealogy', *Lancashire* **15**(1), 1994, 25-32.
   Reprint of a Public Record Office leaflet.
Ships musters series 1 & 2, ADM 36 & 37. List
   and Index Society **248-9**. 1992. Lists ships
   muster books, 1688-1842.
The Royal Naval Museum at Portsmouth is
another important library. Brief discussions of
its collections include:
ARMSTRONG, MICHAEL. 'The Royal Naval
   Museum, Portsmouth', *Family tree magazine*
   8(2), 1991, 41.
TROTMAN, ANDREW. 'The Royal Naval Museum,
   Portsmouth: genealogy at the King Alfred
   Library and Reading Room', *Genealogists'
   magazine* **24**(5), 1993, 197-9.
'Royal Naval Museum: the King Alfred Library
   and Reading Room', *Isle of Wight Family
   History Society [journal]* **23**, 1991, 11-13.

Seamen (Royal Navy) *continued*

Many naval papers are now in North America; see:

MORRISS, ROGER. *Guide to British naval papers in North America.* Mansell Publishing, 1994. Extensive; published in cooperation with the National Maritime Museum.

Numerous original documents of naval interest have been published in:

Navy Records Society publications. The Society, 1894- .

Many biographical dictionaries and lists of naval personnel are available; for comprehensive details, especially on the various naval lists, see the National Maritime Museum *Catalogue* mentioned above. The history of the various official and semi-official navy lists is outlined in:

PERRIN, W.G. 'The Navy List', *Mariners mirror* 1, 1911, 257-64 & 321-9.

The selected lists and other works noted below are arranged in rough chronological order:

HEWITT, H.J. *The organization of war under Edward III 1338-62.* [Manchester]: Manchester University Press, 1966. Appendix lists masters of ships used as troop carriers, 1345.

ANDERSON, R.C. *List of English naval captains, 1642-1660.* Occasional Publications, **8**. Society for Nautical Research, 1964.

MERRIMAN, REGINALD DUNDAS, ed. *The Sergison papers.* Publications, **89**. Navy Records Society, 1950. Includes various lists of naval officers, clerks, etc., 17-18th c.

SYRETT, DAVID, & DINARDO, R.L., eds. *The commissioned sea officers of the Royal Navy 1660-1815.* Navy Records Society, 1995. This is an extensive revision of a work of the same title by David Bonner-Smith published in 3 vols., National Maritime Museum, 1954.

A complete list of the Royal Navy ... D.Steel, 1780-1806. Irregular; title varies. Frequently referred to as *Steel's list of the Royal Navy.*

CHARNOCK, J. *Biographia navalis, or impartial memoirs of the lives and characters of officers of the navy of Great Britain from the year 1660 to the present time.* 6 vols. R. Faulder, 1794-8.

DAVIES, J.D. *Gentlemen and tarpaulins: the officers and men of the Restoration navy.* Oxford: Clarendon Press, 1991. Includes a good bibliography.

DALTON, CHARLES, ed. *List of half-pay officers (English establishment) 1714.* Eyre & Spottiswoode, 1900.

A list of the flag officers and other comissioned officers of His Majesty's fleet, with the dates of their respective commissions. Admiralty Office, 1787-1837. Annual; title varies.

A list of the officers of His Majesty's marine forces ... Admiralty Office, 1790-1827. Irregular; title varies.

RALFE, J. *The naval biography of Great Britain, consisting of memoirs of those officers of the British Navy who distinguished themselves during the reign of His Majesty George III.* 4 vols. Whitmore & Fenn, 1828. Includes about 150 biographies.

Steel's original and correct list of the Royal Navy ... Steel, 1782-1816. Published monthly at first, then quarterly; lists all officers. Superseded by the official *Navy list.*

The Naval chronicle. 34 vols. Bunney & Gold, 1799-1818. Lists births, marriages, & deaths, appointments, etc. A modern index is provided by: HURST, NORMAN. *Naval Chronicle, 1799-1818: index to births marriages and deaths.* Coulsdon: the author, 1989.

Navy list. H.M.S.O., et al, 1814- . Annual; lists officers. For full details of this work and its various supplements, consult the National Maritime Museum's *Catalogue.*

MACKENZIE, ROBERT HOLDEN. *The Trafalgar roll, containing the names and services of all officers of the Royal Navy and the Royal Marines, who participated in the glorious victory of the 21st October 1805, together with a history of the ships engaged in the battle.* George Allen & Co., 1913. Includes brief biographical notes.

MARSHALL, JOHN. *Royal Navy biography, or memoirs of the services of all the flag-officers, superannuated rear-admirals, retired-captains, post-captains, and commanders, whose names appeared on the Admiralty list of sea officers at the commencement of the present year, or who have since been promoted.* 4 vols. in 8. Longman, Hurst, Rees, Orme & Brown, 1823-35. 4 vol. supplement, including biographies of post-captains only, 1827-30.

Seamen (Royal Navy) *continued*

A list of the masters, medical officers and pursers of His Majesty's Fleet, with the dates of their first warrants. H.M.S.O., 1827-30. 3 issues. Publisher varies.

O'BYRNE, WILLIAM R. *A naval biographical dictionary, comprising the life and services of every living officer in Her Majesty's navy, from the rank of Admiral of the Fleet to that of Lieutenant, inclusive, compiled from authentic and family documents.* John Murray, 1849. Lives of some 5,000 naval officers. A new edition was published in 1861, but is incomplete.

CATTY, MERYL. *Certificates and declarations for placing widows of officers of the Royal Navy on the pension list: index of officers from pension forms in ADM 1, Promiscuous letters, 1846-65, inc.* 1 fiche. [ ], 1991.

The active lists of flag officers and captains of the Royal Navy, with particulars exhibiting the progress &c., of officers from their entry into the service. Edward Stanford, 1861.

ARTHUR, WILLIAM, & GRIFFIN, JAMES. *The active list of flag officers, captains, commanders & lieutenants of the Royal Navy, with particulars exhibiting the progress &c., of officers from their entry into the service to June 30, 1868.* Portsea: Griffin & Co., 1868.

1876: the active list of flag officers, captains, commanders & senior lieutenants of the Royal Navy, with particulars exhibiting the progress &c., of officers ... Portsmouth: Griffin & Co., [1876]. Further issues were published in 1879 and 1883.

The Royal Navy list ... Witherby & Co., et al., 1878-1917. Title varies; often referred to as *Lean's Royal Navy list.*

1881 census ... index: Royal Navy. 11 fiche. [F.F.H.S.,] [1993?] Full index; important.

CAPPER, H.D. *Royal Naval warrant officers annual 1893-94, being a compendium of information for officers of and from that rank, containing list of all active officers, also retired, with their war and meritorious services ...* Economic Printing & Publishing Co., 1894. A further volume was published for 1894-5.

Whitakers naval and military directory and Indian Army list 1899, containing an alphabetical list of commissioned officers on the active list of both services, together with all senior retired officers, with particulars concerning them ... J.Whitaker & Sons, 1899.

Naval war services of officers of the Royal Navy, Royal Naval Reserve, Royal Naval Air Service, Royal Naval Volunteer Reserve, and Royal Marine forces, and a diary of events of the war connected with the Royal Navy. Office of the Royal Navy List, 1917. Alphabetical listing.

Some more specialist lists include:

EDYE, L. 'The English and Spanish fleets of 1588', *Western antiquary* 7, 1887-8, 301-10. List of ships, with names of captains.

Commanders in H.M.Packet Service from 1688 to 1852. Falmouth: J.H.Lake & Co., 1898. List of those appointed by the General Post Office, and by the Admiralty; also includes list of agents at Falmouth.

MARKHAM, CLEMENTS R. *The Arctic navy list, or, a century of Arctic & Antarctic officers, 1773-1873, together with a list of the 1875 expedition and their services.* Griffin & Co., 1875.

BRIANT, JOYCE E. 'Ice blaster', *Hampshire family historian* 15(1), 1988, 30-32. List of naval sledging party who searched for Franklin's Arctic expedition, 1854.

The Engineer officers' navy list and hand-book of information for the Steam Branch of the Royal Navy, January 1869. Devonport: John R.H. Spry, 1869. Includes 'Alphabetical list of engineer officers, with dates of entry and promotion'.

The Royal Navy list, or Who's who in the navy: special war supplement. Witherby & Co., 1917. Biographical information on officers services and honours, 4th August 1914 to 5 December 1915.

Royal Naval Division roll of honour: Drake Battallion. Imperial War Museum, 1993. For 1914-18.

Royal Naval Division roll of honour: Hawke Battallion. Imperial War Museum, 1993. For 1914-18.

Royal Naval Division roll of honour: Hood Battallion. Imperial War Museum, 1991.For 1914-18.

Medals

The study of naval medals may be rewarding to the genealogist; see:

Naval and Air Force honours and awards. J.B.Hayward & Son, [1975]. Various facsimile reprints from the *Navy list* and the *Airforce list.*

DOUGLAS-MORRIS, KENNETH. *Naval medals, 1793-1856.* Privately printed, 1987. Brief notes on medallists.

DOUGLAS-MORRIS, K.G. *The Naval General Service Medal roll, 1793-1840.* London Stamp Exchange, [1986]. Extensive; lists recipients.

DOUGLAS-MORRIS, KENNETH. *Naval long service medals, 1830-1990.* Privately printed, 1991. Lists recipients.

FEVYER, W.H., & WILSON, J.W. *The Africa General Service Medal to the Royal Navy & Royal Marines.* London Stamp Exchange, 1990. Lists recipients.

FEVYER, W.H., & WILSON, J.W. *The Queen's South Africa Medal to the Royal Navy and Royal Marines.* Spink & Son, 1983. List of medallists, 1899-1902.

FEVYER, W.H., & WILSON, J.W. *The China War medal 1900 to the Royal Navy and Royal Marines.* London Stamp Exchange, 1985.

Naval honours and awards, 1939-1940. Geoffrey Bles, 1942. Lists recipients.

MCINNES, IAN. *The Meritorious Service Medal to naval forces.* Chippenham: Picton Publishing, 1983. Lists recipients.

SCARLETT, R.J. *The naval good shooting medal, 1903-1914.* London Stamp Exchange, 1990. Includes roll of recipients, *etc.*

TURNER, JOHN FRAYNE. *V.C.'s of the Royal Navy.* George G.Harrap, 1956. How 24 naval men won the V.C.

WINTON, JOHN. *The Victoria Cross at sea.* Michael Joseph, 1978. Covers 1854-1945.

[DICKSON, W.C.] *Seedie's list of coastal forces awards for World War II.* Tisbury: Ripley Registers, 1992.

[DICKSON, W.C.] *Seedie's list of submarine awards for World War II.* Tisbury: Ripley Registers, 1990.

[DICKSON, W.C.] *Seedie's roll of naval honours & awards, 1939-1959.* Tisbury: Ripley Registers, 1989.

Memorials

IMPERIAL WAR GRAVES COMMISSION. *Naval memorials in the United Kingdom, 1939-1945: introduction to the registers.* Imperial War Graves Commission, 1952. Reprinted with amendments, Maidenhead: Commonwealth War Graves Commission, 1982.

IMPERIAL WAR GRAVES COMMISSION. *Memorials to the naval ranks and ratings of the Commonwealth who fell in the Great War and have no other grave than the sea: the register of the names inscribed on the memorial at the port of Chatham.* 5 pts. Imperial War Graves Commission, 1924. Reprinted with amendments, Maidenhead: Commonwealth War Graves Commission, 1981-6.

IMPERIAL WAR GRAVES COMMISSION. *Memorials to the naval ranks and ratings of the Commonwealth who fell in the Great War and have no other grave than the sea: the register of the names inscribed on the memorial at the port of Plymouth.* 5 pts. Imperial War Graves Commission, 1924. Reprinted with amendments, Maidenhead: Commonwealth War Graves Commission, 1984-8.

IMPERIAL WAR GRAVES COMMISSION. *Memorials to the naval ranks and ratings of the Commonwealth who fell in the Great War and have no other grave than the sea: the register of the names inscribed on the memorial at the port of Portsmouth.* 7 pts. Imperial War Graves Commission, 1924. Reprinted with amendments, Maidenhead: Commonwealth War Graves Commission, 1983-7.

IMPERIAL WAR GRAVES COMMISSION. *The war dead of the British Commonwealth and Empire: the register of those who fell in the 1939-1945 war and have no other grave than the sea: Chatham naval memorial.* Imperial War Graves Commission, 1952.

IMPERIAL WAR GRAVES COMMISSION. *War dead of the British Commonwealth: the register of those who fell in the 1939-1945 war and have no other grave than the sea: Portsmouth naval memorial.* 6 pts. Imperial War Graves Commission, 1953. Reprinted with amendments, Maidenhead: Commonwealth War Graves Comission, 1982-3.

See also Chaplains and Soldiers

Sergeants at Arms

SITWELL, H.D.W. 'Royal Sergeants-at-Arms, and the royal maces', *Archaeologia*, **120**, 1969, 203-50. Includes list, 15-20th c.

Serjeants at Law
See Lawyers

Servants
COLDHAM, PETER WILSON. *The Bristol registers of servants sent to foreign plantations 1654-1686.* Baltimore: Genealogical Publishing, 1988. Records 10,000 emigrants, mainly from the West Country, Wales and the West Midlands. Supersedes R.Hargreave-Mawdsley's *Bristol and America ... 1929.*

HORN, PAMELA. *The rise and fall of the Victorian servant.* Dublin: Gill & Macmillan, 1975. General study; useful bibliography.

MUNBY, ARTHUR J., *Faithful servants: epitaphs and obituaries recording their names and services.* Reeves & Turner, 1891. Arranged topographically.

'Notes on sources 6: returns of emigrating indentured servants', *Lancashire [Rossendale Society for Genealogy & Heraldry journal]* 3(12), 1982, 13. Brief note on sources for servants emigrating to Virginia, Maryland and Pennsylvania.

Shareholders
'Was your ancestor a shareholder?' *Family History Society of Cheshire [journal]* 18(2), 1988, 11-12. Brief note on the Companies Registration Office.

The names and descriptions of the proprietors of unclaimed dividends on the publick funds, transferable at the South-Sea House, which became due before the 31st December 1780, and remained unpaid the 31st December 1790 ... South Sea Company, [1791?]

The names and descriptions of the proprietors of all government funds and securities transferable at the Bank of England whose stock and dividends have been transferred for the reduction of the national debt, in pursuance of the Act of the 56th Geo. III, Cap.60, as unclaimed for ten years and upwards, since the date of the last publication in 1823, to 5th January 1836 ... Teape & Jones, 1836. Further vols. published 1838, 1841 and 1842.

Sheriffs
GREEN, JUDITH A. *English sheriffs to 1154.* Public Record Office handbook, 24. H.M.S.O., 1990.

List of sheriffs for England and Wales from the earliest times to 1831, compiled from documents in the Public Record Office. Lists and indexes, 9. New York: Kraus Reprint, 1963. Originally published H.M.S.O., 1896. The reprint includes many manuscript notes from the copy kept in the Public Record Office.

PAYEN-PAYNE, J.BERTRAND. *The roll of the high sheriffs of England and Wales for the year of grace 1877, recording the arms and the lineages of those families whose members have been appointed by her most gracious Majesty to serve the honourable office of high sheriffs of their respective counties for the current year.* The author, 1878. Includes heraldic notes and extensive pedigrees.

HARTLEY, J.E. 'Under-sheriffs and bailiffs in some English shrievalties c.1580 to c.1625', *Bulletin of the Institute of Historical Research* 47, 1974, 164-85. Includes various lists for Derbyshire, Cambridgeshire, Essex, Huntingdonshire, Hertfordshire, Kent, Staffordshire and Worcestershire.

Shipbuilders
RITCHIE, L.A., ed. *The shipbuilding industry: a guide to historical records.* Manchester: Manchester University Press, 1992.

RITCHIE, L.A. *Modern British shipbuilding: a guide to historical records.* Maritime monographs & reports, 48. National Maritime Museum, 1980. Includes information on records of shareholders and staff, which may be of genealogical value.

See also Seamen (Mercantile Marine)

Shipowners
CRAIG, ROBERT. 'Shipping records of the nineteenth and twentieth centuries', *Archives* 7(36), 1966, 191-8. General discussion.

DAVIES, REGINALD. 'Certificates of British registry of vessels: an unusual genealogical source', *Family tree magazine* 9(11), 1993, 21-2.

DAVIS, RALPH. 'Shipping records', *Archives* 7(35), 1966, 135-42. General discussion.

JARVIS, R.C. 'Sources for the history of ships and shipping', *Journal of transport history* 3, 1957-8, 212-34. May be useful if you are searching for shipowners.

JONES, CLEMENT WAKEFIELD, SIR. *Pioneer shipowners.* 2 vols. Liverpool: C. Birchall & Sons, 1935-9. 26 biographies.

MATHIAS, P., & PEARSALL, A.W.H. *Shipping: a survey of historical records.* Newton Abbot: David & Charles, 1971. Lists archives of shipping companies, including many staff records; also lists records held in county and other record offices, with names of ships and owners or masters, etc.

The directory of shipowners, shipbuilders and marine engineers. Directory Publishing Co., 1903- . Includes directors' names of shipping companies.

The shipping world year book. The Shipping World, 1887- . Annual. Some issues include a 'who's who'.

See also Seamen (Mercantile Marine)

Shipwrights
SPILER, MARGARET. 'The shipwright', *Family tree magazine* 8(7), 1994, 4-5; 8(8), 1992, 4-5.

Shoemakers
VICKERS, R.L. 'Old occupations: shoemaking', *Family tree magazine* 9(12), 1993, 32-3.

Shop Workers
POOLE, LORNA. 'British business archives, I: the John Lewis partnership', *Business archives* 37, 1972, 11-16. Brief description of archives, some of which relate to employees.

Silversmiths
FERGUSON, ANN. 'Silversmiths and hallmarks', *Family tree magazine* 11(4), 1995, 36-7.

GLANVILLE, PHILIPPA. *Silver in England.* Unwin Hyman, 1987. Includes extensive bibliography.

GRANVILLE, PHILIPPA, & GOLDSBOROUGH, JENNIFER FAULDS. *Women silversmiths 1685-1845: works from the collection of the National Museum of Women in the Arts, Washington, D.C.* Thames and Hudson, 1990. Includes a 'biographical list' of 300 women — two-thirds of them from London.

MACDONALD-TAYLOR, MARGARET. *A dictionary of marks,* revised by Lucilla Watson. Rev.ed. Barrie & Jenkins, 1992. Gives many names of silversmiths, goldsmiths, pewterers, potters, furniture makers, etc.

WYLER, SEYMOUR B. *The book of old silver: English, American, foreign, with all available hallmarks, including Sheffield plate marks.* 2nd.ed. New York: Crown Publishers, 1937.

See also Goldsmiths

Smugglers
DERRIMAN, JAMES. 'Smugglers, customs men and privateers', *Cornwall Family History Society journal* 56, 1990, 21-6.

LODEY, JOY. 'Was your ancestor a smuggler?' *Family tree magazine* 5(11), 1989, 3-4.

Soapmakers
VICKERS, RAY. 'Old occupations: soapmakers', *Family tree magazine* 9(6), 1993, 4-5.

The soap makers directory, being a list of the manufacturers of soap in Great Britain, with some of those in Ireland. Saml. Harris & Co., 1888-1955. 58 issues. Alphabetical list; the 6th and successive issues also include a 'list of candle makers in Great Britain'.

Soldiers
The present generation of Englishmen is the first which has not been liable for 'national service'. The obligation to defend the community has been recognised since Anglo-Saxon times, and consequently a very high proportion of our ancestors can be traced in military records — even if they only served in the 'Dad's army' of the volunteers. The literature on soldiering is enormous; archival resources are even more extensive. It is planned to publish a separate volume in the *British genealogical bibliographies* series to provide in-depth coverage of the available literature. The information provided here is consequently very selective, and primarily identifies works written specifically for genealogists and other researchers. The standard work on army ancestry for genealogists, strongest on commissioned ranks, is:

HAMILTON-EDWARDS, GERALD. *In search of army ancestry.* Phillimore, 1977.

See also:

GRAY, ERIK A. 'The British regular army and its records 1660-1913', *Family history news and digest* 8(2), 1991, 63-6.

Soldiers *continued*

WATTS, M.J., & WATTS, C.T. *My ancestor was in the British army: how can I find out more about him?* Society of Genealogists, 1992.

For further information on published works, consult the following bibliographies:

BRUCE, ANTHONY. *A bibliography of the British army, 1660-1914.* 2nd ed. K.G. Saur, 1985. Lists many biographies, regimental histories, guides to source materials, etc.

HIGHAM, ROBIN, ed. *A guide to the sources of British military history.* Routledge & Kegan Paul, 1972. Standard bibliography.

Supplemented by:

JORDAN, GERALD, ed. *British military history: a supplement to Robin Higham's 'Guide to the sources'* New York: Garland Publishing, 1988.

For volunteers, see:

WHITE, A.S., & MARTIN, ERNEST J. 'A bibliography of volunteering', *Journal of the Society for Army Historical Research* **23**, 1945, 8-25.

An index to an important journal, which carries many articles of potential relevance, is provided by:

Journal of the Society for Army Historical Research: general index, volumes I-XL, 1921-1962. Robert Stockwell for the Society, 1969. Detailed subject index, including names, & index of regiments.

For a basic introduction to sources at the Public Record Office, see:

Records of officers and soldiers who have served in the British Army. 2nd ed. Public Record Office, 1985.

Muster books and pay lists, general series, Cavalry, (W012/1-13305). List & Index Society, **210**. 1984. List of records, 18-19th c., at the Public Record Office.

List of War Office records preserved in the Public Record Office Public Record Office lists and indexes **28**. Amended ed. New York: Kraus Reprint, 1963. Identifies innumerable lists *etc.* of soldiers.

World Wars I & II

Most of us have relatives who fought in the two world wars. The standard guide for genealogists to sources for World War I army ancestry is:

HOLDING, NORMAN. *World War I army ancestry.* 2nd ed. Birmingham: F.F.H.S., 1991.

See also:

HOLDING, N.H. *More sources of World War I army ancestry.* 2nd ed. F.F.H.S., 1991.

HOLDING, NORMAN. *The location of British army records: a national directory of World War I sources.* Plymouth: F.F.H.S., 1984. Include listing by county, with many bibliographical notes.

Innumerable works have been written on the two world wars; many are identified in:

BAYLISS, GWYN M. *Bibliographical guide to the two world wars: an annotated survey of English language reference material.* Bowker, 1977. See especially the section on 'Biographies', 313-57.

ENSER, A.G.S. *A subject bibliography of the First World War: books in English, 1914-1987.* Aldershot: Gower, 1979.

ENSER, A.G.S. *A subject bibliography of the Second World War: books in English, 1939-1974.* Andre Deutsch, 1977. A supplement covers books published 1975-83.

For archival materials, consult:

MAYER, S.L., & KEONIG, W.J. *The two world wars: a guide to manuscript collections in the United Kingdom.* Bowker, 1976. Lists many papers giving biographical information, including, for example, diaries, lists of officers, regimental histories, etc.

The Second World War: a guide to documents in the Public Record Office. Public Record Office handbooks, 11. H.M.S.O., 1972.

Regiments

Many regimental histories contain lists of officers and men, battle honours, etc., all of which are useful. To identify them, see:

WHITE, ARTHUR S. *A bibliography of regimental histories of the British army.* Society for Army Historical Research, 1965.

The Militia, Volunteers, etc.

The regular army is not to be confused with the part-time forces of the militia, volunteers, *etc.* Until the 19th century, most men were liable to be pressed into service in these forces. Genealogists have cause to be grateful for the lists which result. Surviving muster rolls for the 16th and 17th centuries, naming able-bodied men in the places covered are listed in:

GIBSON, J.S.W., & DELL, A. *Tudor and Stuart muster rolls: a directory of holdings in the British Isles.* Birmingham: F.F.H.S., 1989 (updated 1991).

The essential guide to records of the modern militia is:

THOMAS, GARTH. *Records of the militia from 1757, including records of the Volunteers, Rifle Volunteers, Yeomanry, Fencibles, Territorials, and the Home Guard.* Public Record Office readers' guide, 3. PRO Publications, 1993.

Surviving militia ballot lists are identified in:

GIBSON, J.S.W., & MEDLYCOTT, M.T. *Militia lists and musters: a directory of holdings in the British Isles.* 3rd ed. F.F.H.S., 1994.

Army lists

Innumerable lists of army personnel have been published. A comprehensive guide to these lists is provided by:

LESLIE, J.H., et al. 'Old printed army lists', *Journal of the Society of Army Historical Research* 1, 1921-2, 6-9, 56-9 & 142-5; **2**, 1923, 164-7; **3**, 1924, 22-5 & 85-8. See also **9**, 1930, 147-61 & 214-42.

See also East India Men and Medical men

Solicitors

See Lawyers

South Sea Company Proprietors

Accounts presented to the House of Commons pursuant to their orders of 20th May 1805, relating to the South Sea Company's unclaimed dividends. House of Commons Parliamentary Papers 1806, **XII**, 13-103. Extensive list of shareholders who had not claimed their dividends, dating back to the early 18th c.

Speakers

ROSKELL, J.S. *Parliament and politics in late medieval England.* 3 vols. Hambledon Press, 1981-3. Vols. 2-3 are devoted to biographies of medieval speakers of the House of Commons.

Spies

FOWLER, SIMON. 'Tinker, tailor, soldier, spy', *Family tree magazine* 11(5), 1995, 18-19. Sources for spies.

Spoonmakers

SNODIN, MICHAEL. *English silver spoons.* Charles Letts and Co., 1974. Includes names of spoon-makers, also a useful bibliography.

Sportsmen

Burke's who's who in sport and sporting records 1922. The Burke Publishing Co., 1922.

Who's who in sport: an authoritative reference guide to sport and sportsmen. Shaw Publishing, 1935.

See also Cricketers, Golfers, Huntsmen, Jockeys, Rugby Players and Tennis Players.

Stamp Collectors and Dealers

BIRTWHISTLE, GEORGE. *The directory of foreign stamp collectors, 1883.* Seacombe: George Birtwhistle, 1883. i.e. collectors of foreign stamps.

The British stamp directory. Birmingham: Hill, Barton & Co., 1881. Lists stamp dealers.

BARKER, W.E., & MORGAN, R.T. *The British & colonial philatelic directory of dealers and collectors.* Sheffield: W.E.Barker, 1900.

The philatelists register 1902. Boscombe: C.J.Endle & Co., 1901-2.

The imperial stamp directory. Ipswich: Geo.I.Spalding, [1881]. Lists stamp dealers and collectors.

NUNN, C.H. *The stamp dealers of Great Britain, being a directory containing the names and addresses of nearly every stamp dealer in Great Britain, to which are added the names and addresses of several collectors, and numerous advertisements, &c.* Bury St. Edmunds. C.H.Nunn, 1880-92. 4 issues. Continued by: *Nunn's directory: the stamp dealers of Great Britain.* 1892-1900. 9 issues.

Who's who in philately. Philatelic Circular, 1914-37. Annual. Publisher varies.

Stationers

See Booksellers

Statisticians

STATISTICAL SOCIETY OF LONDON. *List of the fellows of the Statistical Society of London.* W.Clowes, 1834. Lists of fellows are included in the Society's *journal*, 1876-1915.

Stewards

HAINSWORTH, D.R. *Stewards, lords and people: the estate steward and his world in later Stuart England.* Cambridge: C.U.P., 1992. General study, with a useful 'note on the manuscript sources'.

Stockbrokers

List of members of the Stock Exchange ... E.Couchman & Co., *et al.* 1850- .

Ralph's stock and share brokers directory for 185-, giving the business addresses of the members of the London Stock Exchange, and provincial exchanges of Birmingham, Bristol, Dublin, Edinburgh, Glasgow, Hull, Leeds, Liverpool, Manchester, Sheffield and York. Longman, Brown, Green & Longmans, 1852-7. Annual.

The stockbrokers directory of Great Britain and Ireland. Geo. S. Smith & Co., 1873-4.

Students and Scholars *etc.*

Every reader of this book went to school, and records of our schooling probably survive in the archives. This is not necessarily so for earlier generations; however, for a brief discussion of educational records, see:

WOOD, TOM. 'Did your ancestor go to school?' *Family tree magazine* 7(9), 1991, 15-16.

Many registers of the universities, colleges and schools of Britain have been published, and only a few can be listed here. Detailed listings are provided in two works:

JACOBS, PHYLLIS MAY. *Registers of the universities, colleges and schools of Great Britain and Ireland: a list.* Athlone Press, 1966.

School, university and college registers in the library of the Society of Genealogists. The Society, 1988

A discussion of sources for editors of school registers is provided by:

WICKS, A.T. 'School registers', *Amateur historian* 4,(1), 1958, 29-33.

Until the nineteenth century, most English students studied at Oxford or Cambridge (or at the Inns of Court — see 'Lawyers'). Many of the benefactors of these — and other — institutions are identified in:

G[ILBERT], R. *Liber scholasticus, or, an account of the fellowships, scholarships and exhibitions at the Universities of Oxford and Cambridge, by whom founded, and whether open to natives of England and Wales or restricted to particular places and persons; also of such colleges, public schools, endowed grammar schools, chartered companies of the City of London, corporate bodies, trustees, &c., as have university advantages attached to them or in their patronage.* E.J.G. & F.Rivington, 1829.

Cambridge University

Every genealogist should consult Venn's listing of Cambridge alumni:

VENN, J., & VENN, J.A. *Alumni Cantabrigienses.* Cambridge: C.U.P., 1922-54. Pt.1. (1250-1751). (4 vols). Pt.2. 1751-1900. (6 vols).

A number of works are available to supplement this listing:

COOPER, CHARLES HENRY. & COOPER, THOMPSON. *Athenae Cantabrigienses.* 3 vols. Cambridge: Deighton Bell & Co., 1858-1913. v.1. 1500-1585. v.2. 1586-1609. v.3. 1609-1611, additions and corrections, index.

EMDEN, A.B. *A biographical register of the University of Cambridge to 1500.* Cambridge: C.U.P., 1963.

NEALE, C.M. *Early honour lists of University of Cambridge.* Bury St Edmunds: F.T. Groom & Son, 1909. Covers 1498-1747.

TANNER, J.R. *The historical register of the University of Cambridge, being a supplement to the calendar, with a record of University offices, honours and distinctions to the year 1910.* Cambridge: C.U.P., 1917. Supplements appear regularly.

VENN, JOHN, & VENN, J.A. *The book of matriculations and degrees: a catalogue of those who have been matriculated or been admitted to any degree in the University of Cambridge from 1544 to 1659.* Cambridge: C.U.P., 1913. Works of the same title are also available for subsequent periods.

Oxford University

The major listing for Oxford, which is also required reading, is:

FOSTER, JOSEPH. *Alumni Oxonienses: the members of the University of Oxford, 1500-1714, their parentage, birthplace, and year of birth, with a record of their degrees, being the matriculation register of the University, alphabetically arranged, revised and annotated.* 4 vols. Oxford: James Parker & Co., 1891. A further 4 vols., published in 1888, cover the years 1715-1886.

See also:

BOASE, C.W. & CLARK, ANDREW. *Register of the University of Oxford.* 2 vols in 5. Oxford Historical Society **1, 10-12 & 14.** Oxford: the Society, 1884-9. v.l. 1449-63; 1505-71. v.2. 1571-1622. The official record of matriculations, degrees, etc.

BURROWS, MONTAGU, ed. *The register of the visitors of the University of Oxford, from A.D. 1647 to A.D. 1658.* Camden new series, **29.** Camden Society, 1881. Includes much useful information on members of the University.

EMDEN, A.B. *A biographical register of the University of Oxford to A.D. 1500.* 3 vols. Oxford: Clarendon Press, 1957-9. For corrections and additions, see *Bodleian Library Record* **6,** 1957-61, 668-88, & **7,** 1962-7, 149-64.

EMDEN, A.B. *A biographical register of the University of Oxford A.D. 1501 to 1540.* Oxford: Clarendon Press, 1974. For corrections, see Margaret Bowker's review in *Archives* 12(53), 1975, 15-24.

FOSTER, JOSEPH. *Oxford men, 1880-1892, with a record of their schools, honours and degrees.* Oxford: John Parker & Sons, 1893. Continuation of *Alumni Oxoniensis.*

FOSTER, JOSEPH. *Oxford men and their colleges.* Oxford: J. Parker, 1893. Supplements *Alumni Oxoniensis* with biographical notes on all heads and fellows of colleges.

WOOD, ANTHONY A. *Athenae Oxonienses: an exact history of all the writers and bishops who have had their education in the University of Oxford, to which are added, the fasti, or annals, of the said University.* New ed. 5 vols. F.C. & J. Rivington, 1813-20. A later edition was commenced in 1848 by the Ecclesiastical History Society, but not completed. Includes numerous biographies.

Many more works of genealogical interest are listed in:

CORDEAUX, E.H., & MERRY, D.H. *A bibliography of printed works relating to the University of Oxford.* Oxford: Clarendon Press, 1968.

Other Universities

Some of the younger universities have also published lists of their members. For two examples, see:

Exeter University register, 1893-1962: a register of officers, officials, staff, graduates and holders of diplomas, certificates and testamurs. Exeter: University of Exeter, 1970.

MANCHESTER UNIVERSITY. *Register of graduates and holders of diplomas and certificates, 1851-1958.* Manchester: Manchester U.P., 1959. Supplements issued regularly.

Some English students went to Dublin, and may be traced in:

BURTCHAELL, GEORGE DAWE, & SADLEIR, THOMAS ULICK, eds. *Alumni Dublinensis: a register of the students, graduates, professors, and provosts of Trinity College, in the University of Dublin.* Williams & Norgate, 1924.

A catalogue of graduates who have proceeded to degrees in the University of Dublin from the earliest recorded commencements to July 1866, with supplement to December 16, 1868. Dublin: Hodges, Smith & Foster, 1869.

English speaking students at Leyden and Louvain are listed in:

PEACOCK, EDWARD. *Index to English speaking students who have graduated at Leyden University.* Index Society publications **13.** Longmans, Green & Co., 1883.

VOCHT, H.DE. 'Excerpts from the register of Louvain University from 1485 to 1527', *English historical review* **37,** 1922, 89-105.

See also Teachers

Students and Scholars (Roman Catholic)

Douai

HARRIS, P.R. *Douai College documents, 1639-1794.* Catholic Record Society Publications (Records series) **63.** 1972. Includes various lists of students, *etc.*

Lisbon

SHARRATT, MICHAEL. *Lisbon College register 1628-1813.* Catholic Record Society publication (records series) **72.** 1991.

Rome

KELLY, WILFRID, et al, eds. *Liber ruber venerabilis collegii Anglorum de urbe.* Publications of the Catholic Record Society 37 & 40. 1940-43. v.1. 1579-1630. v.2. 1631-1783. Register of a college in Rome.

KENNY, ANTHONY, ed. *The responsa scholarum of the English College, Rome.* Publications of the Catholic Record Society. 54-5. 1962-3. Pt.1. 1598-1621. Pt. 2. 1622-1685. Gives brief biographies of Roman Catholic students. See also:

BROOKS, LESLEY. The *Responsa Scholarum* of the English College, Rome', *E.C.A.Journal* 2(6), 1988, 134-7.

St. Omer

HOLT, GEOFFREY. *St. Omers and Bruges colleges 1593-1773: a biographical dictionary.* Catholic Record Society publications (record series) **69**. 1979.

Seville

MURPHY, MARTIN *St. Gregory's College, Seville, 1592-1767.* Catholic Record Society (Records series) **73**. 1992. Lists alumni of this English college.

Valladolid

HENSON,EDWIN, ed. *The registers of the English College at Valladolid, 1589-1862.* Publications of the Catholic Record Society **30**. 1930.

Sugar Refiners

FAIRRIE, GEORFFREY. *The sugar refining families of Great Britain.* Tate & Lyle, 1951. Brief histories of the families of Fairrie, Kerr, Lyle, Macfie, Martineau, Tate and Walker; includes pedigrees 18-19th c.

Surveyors

EDEN, PETER, ed. *Dictionary of land surveyors and land cartographers of Great Britain and Ireland, 1550-1850.* 3 vols. Folkestone: Wm. Dawson, 1975-6. Supplement, 1979.

THOMPSON, F.M.L. *Chartered surveyors: the growth of a profession.* Routledge & Kegan Paul, 1968. Includes 'select, concise, biographical dictionary of surveyors and their associates'.

Register of chartered surveyors, chartered land agents, and of auctioneers & estate agents, published under the sanction of and comprising members of the Chartered Surveyors Institution, the Auctioneers and Estate Agents Institute, the Incorporated Society of Auctioneers and Landed Property Agents. Thomas Skinner & Co., 1937-55. 7 issues.

Teachers

BARR, BARBARA. *Histories of girls' schools and related biographical material: a union list of books in the stock of education libraries in British universities ...* Leicester: Librarians of Institutes and Schools of Education, 1984.

BARTLE, GEORGE F. 'The records of the British and Foreign School Society', *Genealogists magazine* 23(3), 1989, 102-3. Records may be used to follow the careers of individual teachers, and the progress of students.

BEALES, A.C.F. 'A biographical catalogue of Catholic schoolmasters in England from 1558-1700, with an index of places, I: 1558-1603', *Recusant history* **7**, 1964, 268-89.

CHRISTOPHERS, ANN. *An index to nineteenth-century British educational biography.* Education Libraries Bulletin, supplement **10**. University of London Institute of Education, 1965. Lists 450 biographical works.

CUNNINGHAM, PETER. *Local history of education in England and Wales: a bibliography.* Educational Administration and History monograph, **4**. Leeds: University of Leeds Museum of the History of Education, 1976. Lists many school histories, but excludes those listed by Jacobs (see Students) and Wallis (see below).

ROGERS, COLIN D. 'The genealogical uses of education records', *Genealogists' magazine* 21(6), 1984, 202-5. For tracing teachers and students.

STEPHENS, W.B., & UNWIN, R.W. *Materials for the local and regional study of schooling.* Archives and the user **7**. British Records Association, 1987. Detailed discussion of records for the educational historian, which is also suggestive for the genealogist.

SUTHERLAND, GILLIAN. 'A view of education records in the nineteenth and twentieth centuries', *Archives* 15(66), 1981, 79-85. General discussion.

TATE, W.E. 'S.P.C.K. archives, with special reference to their value for the history of education', *Archives* 3(18), 1957, 105-15.

WALLIS, J. *Histories of old schools: a revised list for England and Wales.* Newcastle-Upon-Tyne: University of Newcastle Dept of Education, 1966. For schools in existence prior to 1700. A select list of other school histories is provided in an appendix by:

CURTIS, S.J. *History of education in Great Britain.* 7th ed. University Tutorial Press, 1967.

Crockford's scholastic directory for 1861, being an annual work of reference for facts relating to educators, education, and educational establishments (public and private) in the United Kingdom. John Crockford, 1861. Includes various lists *etc.* of teachers.

The directory of women teachers: a directory of the women engaged in the work of higher and secondary education. Year Book Press, 1913-27. 5 issues; title varies. Biographical dictionary.

'Dissenters schools, 1660-1820', *Transactions of the Baptist Historical Society* 4, 1914-15, 220-27. Lists schoolmasters.

The educational list and directory for 1885: a scholastic guide for the United Kingdom, with a register of schools of art, music, sciences, etc., and professors, tutors, and governesses. F.Evans & Co., 1885. Includes list of 'proprietary and grammar schools', naming their heads.

National Union of Teachers war record, 1914-1919: a short account of duty and work accomplished during the war. Hamilton House, 1920. Includes lists of those who served.

The Schoolmasters yearbook and directory for 19--: a reference book of secondary education in England and Wales. Swan Sonnenschein & Co., 1903-32. Includes lists of schoolmasters and schools.

The Science Masters Association list of members (correct to October 1st 1946). [The Association,] 1946.

Testimonials of masters trained at the National Society's Institution at Battersea ... Privately published, 1848. Prints 92 testimonials to schoolmasters.

'Victorian elementary schools: some notes on sources for family historians', *Ormskirk & District family historian* 2, 1992, 16-17. Brief list of sources for teachers.

See also Cookery Teachers

Temperance Workers

HARRISON, BRIAN. *Dictionary of British temperance biography.* Aids to research, 1. Society for the Study of Labour History, 1973.

HARRISON, BRIAN. 'The British Prohibitionists 1853-1872: a biographical analysis', *International review of social history* 15(3), 1970, 375-467. Includes notes on 234 prohibitionists.

WINSKILL, P.T. *The Temperance Movement and its workers: a record of social, moral, religious and political progress.* 4 vols. Blackie & Sons, 1892. Includes numerous portraits and biographical notices.

Tennis Players

DOREY, H.V. *Who's who in war-time lawn tennis.* Amateur Sports Publishing Co., 1945.

Textile Trades

FARNIE, D.A. 'John Worrall of Oldham, directory-publisher to Lancashire and to the world 1868-1970', *Manchester region history review* 4(1), 1990, 30-5. Includes a list of directories of textile manufacturers.

Kelly's directory of the manufacturers of textile fabric ... Kelly's Directories, 1880-1928. 12 issues. Includes extensive listing of a wide variety of trades, e.g. drapers, tailors, haberdashers, silk manufacturers, outfitters, hosiers, *etc., etc.*

Limitation of Supplies (Woven Textiles) Order 1941: list of persons whose names were, on 1st May 1941, entered on the Limitation of Supplies (Woven Textiles) register. H.M.S.O., 1941.

See also Business Records and Inventors

Tobacco Trades

The directory of the tobacco trade in Great Britain and Ireland, and trade reference book, containing complete lists of all sections of the tobacco trade in nearly every town in the United Kingdom having a population over 5000 ... Tobacco, 1883-1922. 11 issues.

Toilet Trades

The Toilet Preparation (no.3) Order 1943: list of persons whose names were on 1st January entered in parts I and II of the Toilet Preparation register kept by the Board of Trade ... and list of licensed packers. H.M.S.O., 1943.

Tontine Nominees

A list of the nominees appointed by the contributors to the Tontine of the year 1789 ... London: [ ], 1792.

A list of the surviving nominees appointed by the contributors and by the Treasury, to the Tontine of the year 1789 ... National Debt Office, 1868.

A list of the surviving nominees on the fund of survivorship at Midsummer 1730, and their descriptions to that time, also their ages in the year 1693, and the sumes then paid upon each nominees life. Henry King, 1730.

See also Annuitants

Trade Union Records

The records of trade unions — especially membership records - may have genealogical value. Important collections are listed in:

BENNETT, JOHN. *Trade union and related records.* 5th ed. Warwick: University of Warwick Library, 1988.

SAVILLE, JOHN, & DYSON, BRIAN. *The Labour archives at the University of Hull.* Hull: Brynmore Jones Library, 1989.

Brief general discussions are provided by:

STIRK, JEAN. 'A brief survey of trade union records', *North West Kent family history* 7(3), 1995, 79-82.

STOREY, R. 'Records of the working man', *Genealogists' magazine* 20(1), 5-10.

Tradesmen

RUTT, MICHAEL. 'Family history from the billhead', *Family tree magazine* 9(10), 1993, 4-5. Genealogical uses of billheads, trade cards, etc.

Tokens

In an age when coins of low value were in short supply, many tradesmen issued their own tokens. These usually carried their names and sometimes their addresses. The study of them may, therefore, be useful for genealogical purposes. For general discussions, see:

WHITING, J.R.S. *Trade tokens: a social and economic history.* Newton Abbot: David & Charles, 1971. Includes useful bibliography.

BERRY, GEORGE. *Seventeenth century England: traders and their tokens.* Seaby, 1988.

JACOB, KENNETH A. 'Trade tokens and local history', *Amateur historian* 6(2), 1964, 55-61.

Catalogues of a number of major collections of tokens are available:

Catalogue of the Montague Guest collection of badges, tokens, and passes presented in 1907 to the Department of British and Mediaeval Antiquities. British Museum, 1930. Includes lists of tradesmen's tokens *etc.*

GILBERT, W. 'Unpublished seventeenth-century tradesmens' tokens in the collection of William Gilbert', *Numismatic chronicle* 5th series **7**, 1927, 121-55 & 342-69.

GUNSTONE, ANTONY. *Catalogue of the collection of tickets, checks and passes of the nineteenth and twentieth centuries from Great Britain and Ireland.* Leicester: Leicestershire Museums Art Galleries and Records Service, 1984. Lists many tradesmens tokens.

THOMPSON, R.H., et al. *The Norweb collection, Cleveland, Ohio, U.S.A.: tokens of the British Isles, 1575-1750.* Sylloge of Coins of the British Isles, **31, 38, 43, 44** & **46**. Spink & Son, 1984-96. Pt.1. England: Bedfordshire to Devon. Pt.2. Dorset, Durham, Essex and Gloucestershire. Pt.3. Hampshire to Lincolnshire. Pt.4. Norfolk to Somerset. Pt.5. Staffordshire to Westmorland.

SEABY, HERBERT ALLEN & SEABY, PETER JOHN. *A catalogue of the copper coins and tokens of the British Isles.* B.A.Seaby, 1949. Catalogue of a dealer's stock, but lists many tokens, 17-19th c., with names of their issuers.

Many studies of token coinage are available: the following selection is arranged in rough chronological order:

BOYNE, WILLIAM. *Trade tokens issued in the seventeenth century in England, Wales and Ireland, by corporations, merchants, tradesmen, etc.* Rev. ed. by George C. Williamson. 3 vols. B.A. Seaby, 1967. Originally published 1889-91.

KENT, G.C. *British metallic coins and tradesmen's tokens with their value from 1600-1912.* L. Upcott Gill, 1912.

DALTON, R., & HAMER, S.H. *The provincial token coinage of the 18th century illustrated.* B.A. Seaby, 1910. Supplemented by WATERS, ARTHUR W. *Notes on eighteenth century tokens, being supplementary and explanatory notes on The provincial token coinage of the eighteenth century, by Richard Dalton and Samuel H. Hamer.* B.A.Seaby, 1954. Lists innumerable tokens by place.
Unfortunately, there is no index of personal names.

BELL, R.C. *Tradesmen's tickets and private tokens, 1785-1819.* Newcastle-Upon-Tyne: Corbitt & Hunter, 1966.

BELL, R.C. *Commercial coins, 1787-1804.* Newcastle-Upon-Tyne: Corbitt & Hunter, 1963.

MAYS, JAMES O'DONALD. *Tokens of those trying times: a social history of Britain's 19th century silver tokens.* Ringwood: New Forest Leaves, 1991. Useful bibliography.

BELL, R.C. *Copper commercial coins, 1811-1819.* Newcastle-Upon-Tyne: Corbitt & Hunter, 1964.

BELL, R.C. *Unofficial farthings 1820-1870.* Seaby Publications, 1975. Issued by tradesmen.

DALTON, R. *The silver token coinage mainly issued between 1811 and 1812, described and illustrated.* B.A. Seaby, 1968. Originally published 1922.

DAVIS, W.J. *Nineteenth century token coinage.* Spink & Son, 1904. Reprinted Seaby, 1969. Originally published 1969.

Transport Officials and Workers

British transport directory of officials. The Railway Gazette, 1948-49. 2 issues.

JOHNSON, L.C. 'Historical records of the British Transport Commission', *Journal of transport history* 1, 1953-4, 82-96. General description of archives, including staff records. Now out of date. See also *Journal of the Society of Archivists* 1(4), 1956, 94-100.

See also Canal Boatmen, Railwaymen, and Seamen

Tuckers
See Fullers

Upholsterers
See Furniture makers

Valuers
See Auctioneers

Vets

ROYAL COLLEGE OF VETERINARY SURGEONS. *The register of veterinary surgeons from January 1794 to May 1858 inclusive.* The college, 1858. Continued irregularly to 1884, and annually thereafter, under act of Parliament. Title varies.

The veterinary directory, or, annual register of the members of the Royal College of Veterinary Surgeons, besides the unqualified practitioners, in the United Kingdom and the colonies. Edinburgh: Thomas C. Jack, 1861.

Vice-Admirals

MARSDEN, R.G. 'The Vice-Admirals of the coast', *English historical review* 23, 1908, 736-57. List, 16-19th c., by county.

Victuallers

GIBSON, J.S.W., & HUNTER, J. *Victuallers licences.* F.F.H.S., 1991. Written for genealogists.

Violin makers

MORRIS, WILLIAM MEREDITH. *British violin makers: a biographical dictionary of British makers of stringed instruments and bows, and a critical description of their work.* 2nd ed. R. Scott, 1920.

PLOWRIGHT, DENNIS G. *Dictionary of British violin and bow makers.* Exmouth: Dennis G. Plowright, 1994.

Vocalists
See Actors

Watchmakers
See Clockmakers

Water Engineers
BINNIE, G.M. *Early Victorian water engineers.* Thomas Telford, 1981. General discussion of the work of ten water engineers.

Whisky Distillers
BARNARD, ALFRED. *The whisky distilleries of the United Kingdom.* Harper's Weekly Gazette, 1887. Reprinted Newton Abbot: David & Charles, 1969. Gives names of owners, etc.

Wind Instrument Makers
LANGWILL, LYNDESAY G. *An index of musical wind-instrument makers.* 4th ed. Edinburgh: L.G. Langwill, 1974. International, but refers to many British makers.

Wine and Spirit Trades
HARVEY, JAMES. *Wine & spirit trade directory of England & South Wales.* J. Harvey, 1877. Duplicated.

Kelly's directory of the wine and spirit trades, with which are included brewers and maltsters, and other trades connected therewith, of England, Scotland and Wales, and also the principal wine merchants etc. on the continent. 14 vols. Kelly & Co., 1884-1939. Title varies: lists brewers, hoteliers, wine and spirit merchants, hop growers, grocers, *etc., etc.,*

Witches
EWEN, L'ESTRANGE. *Witchcraft and demonism: a concise account derived from sworn depositions and confessions obtained in the courts of England and Wales.* Heath Cranton, 1933. Gives many names, 16-18th c.

Wood Engravers
BUCHANAN-BROWN, JOHN. 'British wood-engravers, c.1820-c.1860: a checklist', *Journal of the Printing Historical Society* 17, 1982-3, 31-62.

Woodworking Trades
NICOLLE, GEORGE. *The woodworking trades: a select bibliography.* Plymouth: Twybill Press, 1994. Lists books on a wide variety of trades, e.g., coopers, planemakers, wheelwrights, *etc.*

Workers
BURNETT, JOHN, VINCENT, DAVID, & MAYALL, DAVID, eds. *The autobiography of the working class: an annotated critical bibliography 1790-1945.* 2 vols. Brighton: Harvester Press, 1984-7. v.1. 1790-1900. v.2. 1900-1945. Lists autobiographies, with biographical notes.

BURNETT, JOHN, ed. *Useful toil: autobiographies of working people from the 1820's to the 1920's.* Allen Lane, 1974. Includes extracts from 26 autobiographies.

Writing Masters
HEAL, AMBROSE. *The English writing masters and their copy books 1570-1800: a biographical dictionary and a bibliography.* Cambridge: C.U.P., 1931.

Yeomen
CAMPBELL, MILDRED. *The English yeoman under Elizabeth and the early Stuarts.* English ed. Merlin Press, 1960. Includes names of many yeomen, and also has a valuable bibliography.

DUDLEY, GEOFFREY A. 'The yeomen of England', *Family tree magazine* 3(2), 1986, 19-20.

Author Index

Surname Index

Place Index